Strategic Studies Institute
and
U.S. Army War College Press

FROM WAR TO DETERRENCE?
ISRAEL-HEZBOLLAH CONFLICT SINCE 2006

Jean-Loup Samaan

May 2014

*****

Comments pertaining to this report are invited and should be forwarded to: Director, Strategic Studies Institute and U.S. Army War College Press, U.S. Army War College, 47 Ashburn Drive, Carlisle, PA 17013-5010.

*****

This manuscript was funded by the U.S. Army War College External Research Associates Program. Information on this program is available on our website, *www.StrategicStudies Institute.army.mil*, at the Opportunities tab.

*****

*****

The Strategic Studies Institute and U.S. Army War College Press publishes a monthly email newsletter to update the national security community on the research of our analysts, recent and forthcoming publications, and upcoming conferences sponsored by the Institute. Each newsletter also provides a strategic commentary by one of our research analysts. If you are interested in receiving this newsletter, please subscribe on the SSI website at *www.StrategicStudiesInstitute.army.mil/newsletter*.

FOREWORD

The 2006 war between Israel and Hezbollah has generated a vast amount of academic and military studies, including a number from the Strategic Studies Institute. Specifically, authors have tried to identify the new patterns of warfare through this conflict and sometimes have even called it the first illustration of "hybrid war." This new monograph by Dr. Jean-Loup Samaan does not look at the war itself but rather at its aftermath, both in Israel and Lebanon. It starts from an obvious paradox: Despite the regional turmoil and the absence of a settlement between Israel and Hezbollah, stability has prevailed since 2006. While over the same time frame the Middle East has been experiencing one of its most unpredictable periods in the last decades, the border area between Israel and Lebanon has remained quiet.

Dr. Samaan explains that this paradox can be understood through the use of deterrence theories. Because both sides understood that a next round would be devastating and that each could not entirely eliminate the threat of retaliation in a first wave of deterrence, the solution has been to bargain deterrence, meaning to deter the other party from attacking its homeland by pledging a full-scale retaliation. To support his claim, Dr. Samaan relies extensively on several field trips in countries, during which he conducted numerous interviews, examined official statements, and gathered grey literature.

Dr. Samaan makes an important contribution to both policy and academic debates over the logic of war between Israel and Hezbollah. In that perspective, his discussion paves the way to a new appraisal of deterrence applied to nonstate actors, as well of escalation dynamics in the Levant. For this reason, the Strategic Studies Institute is pleased to offer this monograph on the role of the U.S. Army and the manner in which it can best serve the nation today and in the future.

DOUGLAS C. LOVELACE, JR.
Director
Strategic Studies Institute and
  U.S. Army War College Press

ABOUT THE AUTHOR

JEAN-LOUP SAMAAN is a researcher for the Middle East Faculty at the North Atlantic Treaty Organization (NATO) Defense College in Rome, Italy. He is a member of the International Institute for Strategic Studies and the Project on Nuclear Issues of the Center for Strategic and International Affairs. His areas of expertise include Middle East strategic balance and Gulf security diplomacies, as well as cyber defense. He was a policy advisor at the French Ministry of Defense from 2008 to 2011 where he was responsible for several net assessment studies covering transatlantic military affairs. While working for the French Ministry of Defense (MoD), he participated in various French-American strategic foresight exercises with the National Intelligence Council as well as with the U.S. Air Force. From 2009 to 2011, he was also an adjunct lecturer in international security at the French Institute for Political Studies, Sciences Program, and gave lectures to civilian and military audiences in various countries. In 2006, he was a visiting scholar at Duke University, and from 2007 to 2008, he was a researcher at the RAND Corporation in Washington, DC. Dr. Samaan has authored three books and several academic articles for various international journals such as *Survival*, *Orbis*, *Comparative Strategy*, *Turkish Policy Quarterly*, *Politique Etrangère*, and *Internationale Politik*. He is a regular columnist for the E-magazine, *Al Monitor*. Dr. Samaan is a former student of Arabic at the French Institute of Oriental Languages and the French Institute for Near East in Beirut, Lebanon. He graduated from the Institute for Political Studies in Grenoble, and holds a Ph.D. in political science from the University of Paris La Sorbonne.

SUMMARY

For 7 years now, the border area between Israel and Lebanon has witnessed calm and stability. At first sight, this has all the appearances of a paradox. The 2006 war between the Israeli Defense Forces (IDF) and the Lebanese organization, Hezbollah, was followed neither by a peace agreement nor by a mere diplomatic process. Both sides prepared their forces to wage the next war and additionally have been confronted in past years to major changes in the distribution of power in the Middle East in the midst of the so-called "Arab Spring."

Against all odds, the area comprising north Israel and south Lebanon remained very quiet these last months. This monograph argues that the key to understand this paradox is the game of deterrence played by both Israel and Hezbollah. Specifically, an informal deterrence dialogue has been developing between Israel and Hezbollah and that strategic stability prevailed because of this indirect exchange.

Because both sides understood that a next round would be devastating and that each could not entirely eliminate the threat of retaliation in a first wave the solution has been to bargain deterrence, meaning to deter the other party from attacking its homeland by pledging a full-scale retaliation.

But to say that stability has been preserved between Israel and Hezbollah thanks to deterrence does not mean that this is a perennial state. This monograph also stresses the precariousness of such deterrence system. The stand-off between Israel and Hezbollah reached this level only through specific measures and conditions that can be reversed in the future. In particular, exogenous factors such as the unraveling of the Syrian civil war or the developments of the Iranian nuclear issue can jeopardize the equilibrium. Moreover, the study of Lebanese politics emphasizes the uncertainties related to the logic of deterrence with a nonstate actor like Hezbollah. This is why this analysis offers a cautious look at deterrence theories in the Middle East and reminds that such situations are neither naturally engendered nor eternally established.

FROM WAR TO DETERRENCE?
ISRAEL-HEZBOLLAH CONFLICT SINCE 2006

INTRODUCTION

For 7 years, the border area between Israel and Lebanon has witnessed calm and stability. At first sight, this state of affairs has all the appearances of a paradox. The 2006 war between the Israeli Defense Forces (IDF) and the Lebanese organization, Hezbollah, was followed neither by a peace agreement nor by a mere diplomatic process. Since then, both sides did not disarm but prepared their forces to wage the next war. The IDF started the planning of a rapid high intensity military campaign targeting South Lebanon and strategic locations inside Beirut (namely its southern suburbs, *Dahya Janoubia*, controlled by Hezbollah). Meanwhile, Hezbollah not only rearmed, but also increased the lethality of its weaponry. Hezbollah also trained its militiamen in a fashion that approached the quality of Special Forces training in neighboring Arab states. In particular, its missile and rocket strike force is now able to reach major urban areas in Israel.

In addition to this arms race, both parties faced critical challenges that could have triggered a new confrontation. In the spring of 2008, Hezbollah prompted an internal conflict in Lebanon with its Sunni competitors that put the country on the brink of a new civil war. Only a few months later, Israel was challenged by rocket salvos on its southern front and conducted Operation CAST LEAD in the Gaza Strip with the objective of destroying the military threat emanating from Hamas and other Palestinian factions.

But overall, Israel and Hezbollah recently have been confronted with major changes to the distribution of power in the Middle East especially during the so-called "Arab Spring." In particular, the revolution in Egypt and the civil war in Syria have been real game changers for both sides as they tested and are still testing the endurance of their regional strategies and their alliances.

Israel pessimistically has assessed the outcomes of the Arab uprisings. A ruler such as Egyptian President Hosni Mubarak, considered to be one of the moderate Arabs in Jerusalem, was replaced by a Muslim Brotherhood-affiliated government in Cairo. Initially marginal during the Arab revolutions, the Brotherhood, as well as the salafists, now represent leading political forces in the Middle East. In the mind of policymakers in Jerusalem, such a regional trend could potentially jeopardize the current status quo with Israel.[1] From the Israeli perspective, the July 2013 military coup in Cairo that toppled Mohammed Morsi only stressed the volatility and instability of the security environment.

With regards to Hezbollah, its two patron states, Iran and Syria, are confronted with close and immediate challenges. As a result of its nuclear program, Iran faces a wide set of international economic sanctions which cripples its economy. Rumors of an Israeli preemptive attack on its nuclear plants regularly resurface and the Gulf monarchies openly aim at Tehran's spheres of influence in the Middle East and the Arabian Peninsula. In Syria, the March 2011 peaceful revolution turned into an all-out war between the rebels and the forces of Bashar al-Assad who eventually dragged Iran and Hezbollah into the fights.

Against this backdrop, common sense would predict that it would take only a slight miscalculation to see Israel and Hezbollah entering into a new conflict, the same way they did in 2006. But this did not happen. Against all odds, the area comprising north Israel and south Lebanon remained very quiet these last months. Hence the question driving this monograph: How did this stability prevail, even though none of the root causes of the conflict had been addressed?

Based on extensive research on the field, this monograph argues that the key to understanding this paradox is the game of deterrence played by both Israel and Hezbollah. Specifically, this analysis explores the very idea that an informal deterrence dialogue has been developing between Israel and Hezbollah and that, in fact, strategic stability — according to Paul Nitze's definition of the terms[2] — prevailed because of this indirect exchange.

In other words, the fact that for the last 7 years both parties prepared themselves to inflict a heavy, if not a fatal, blow to the other is the very reason why no new war has so far erupted. Both sides understood that a next round would be devastating and that each could not entirely eliminate the threat of retaliation in a first wave. Therefore, the solution has been to bargain deterrence, meaning to deter the other party from attacking its homeland by pledging a full-scale retaliation.

But to say that stability has been preserved between Israel and Hezbollah thanks to deterrence does not mean that this is a perennial state. Deterrence works through the combination of factors that can easily be altered, particularly in an evolving regional environment such as the Middle East. The deterrence balance between Israel and Hezbollah as a provisional framework bounded by geographical and socio-political parameters is posited here.

To support the core argument, this monograph is divided into four sections. The first section lays out the theoretical and historical foundations of a deterrence game between Israel and Hezbollah by assessing the role of this concept in their strategic cultures. The second section describes the making of an Israeli military posture vis-à-vis the Party of God in the aftermath of the 2006 war until today. The third section details the parallel developments inside Hezbollah following the so-called "divine victory" of 2006. Finally, the fourth section puts into perspective the deterrence equilibrium between Israel and Hezbollah in the context of current, and possibly future, Middle East crises such as the Syrian civil war and the Iranian nuclear conundrum.

FACTORING DETERRENCE IN THE ISRAEL-HEZBOLLAH CONFRONTATION

Positing the existence of a deterrence system — either loosely or robustly framed — between Israel and Hezbollah since 2006 introduces several assumptions that need to be addressed as prerequisites. In particular, one needs to assess the validity of such concept with regard to the strategic cultures of both Israel and Hezbollah in order to avoid the pitfall of incepting inadequate Western notions.

In fact, a preliminary survey evidences the fact that the word "deterrence" is frequently used both in Israeli military literature and Hezbollah's written documents. For a country that repeatedly resorted to the use of power in its confrontation with regional enemies, Israel may look like an odd applicant for deterrence theories. However, the concept is commonly used by officers and defense intellectuals in interviews as well as in academic research and military doctrines.[3] The reference to the concept of "deterrence" has been salient in the discourse of the Israeli military since the founding of the Jewish State. It can be traced back to David Ben Gurion's rationale for Israeli retaliation policies vis-à-vis the Arabs in the early years of the Israeli state. "Unless we show the Arabs that there is a high price to pay for murdering Jews, we won't survive," said Ben Gurion in 1953.[4] Ben Gurion's statement was the preliminary sketch of an Israeli approach of deterrence by punishment. Two years later, Moshe Dayan, then Chief of staff of the IDF, explained similarly in a speech that:

> We cannot guard every water pipeline from explosion and every tree from uprooting. We cannot prevent every murder of a worker in an orchard or a family in their beds. But it is in our power to set a high price on our blood, a price too high for the Arab community, the Arab army, or the Arab government to think it worth paying.[5]

Both statements of Ben Gurion and Dayan reflect the primary specificity of Israel's approach to deterrence. Contrary to European and American approaches, deterrence in the Israeli strategic culture was never conceived as disconnected from the conduct of military operations, it actually derives from their effectiveness. Whereas western deterrence thinkers distinguish between deterrence posture and warfighting posture, Israeli military planners do not delve into these theoretical discussions. In other words, retaliation against an aggression or a preemptive attack does not mean a failure of deterrence. Retaliation strikes are thought as necessary measures to sustain, on the long haul, the deterrence balance.

A recent illustration of this Israeli specificity is the mainstream discourse within the IDF that followed the 2012 Pillars of Defense operation in the Gaza Strip: it was not portrayed as the result of a failed deterrence system with Hamas and Palestinian factions but as a necessary intervention to restore deterrence.[6] In other words, deterrence is not a pure endstate nor a mere mental construct in Israel's military mentality, it is a cumulative process that includes sporadic clashes to refresh the rules of the game.

This is why some Israeli scholars prefer talking about "cumulative deterrence." Doron Almog, Major General from the Israeli Reserve, explains in the journal, *Parameters*:

> Unlike classical deterrence as practiced during the Cold War, and whose success hinged on a bipolar standoff that held in check any impulse to launch a nuclear first strike, cumulative deterrence is based on the simultaneous use of threats and military force over the course of an extended conflict.[7]

Later in his article, Almog argues against the proponents of classical deterrence thought that consider the use of force as a deterrence failure:

> Cumulative deterrence works on two levels. On the macro level, it seeks to create an image of overwhelming military supremacy. On the micro level, it relies on specific military responses to specific threats or hostile acts. Cumulative deterrence has several key features. First, its effectiveness is measured in terms of the number of victories accumulated over the duration of the conflict, which we can think of as 'assets in a victory bank'. Second, over time these victories produce increasingly moderate behavior on the part of the adversary and a shift in his strategic, operational,

and tactical goals until there is a near-absence of direct conflict. Third, this moderation may eventually result in political negotiations and perhaps even a peace agreement.[8]

The very fact that Israeli decisionmakers do not separate deterrence from the use of force may put into question the relevance of the concept in the first place. When interviewed for this monograph, retired officers were keen on admitting that "Israel does not spend the time Europeans or American spend on discussing and elaborating their theory of deterrence, and to be fair the people who use the word deterrence might not know how to define it."[9] Professor Uri Bar-Joseph stated, "Israeli officers are sometimes confusing the idea of deterrence with simple coercion."[10] Three decades ago, Yoav Ben-Horin and Barry Posen noted likewise that "there has been little systematic, let alone theoretical, elaboration of the concept by Israeli decisionmakers."[11] This is sometimes explained by the fact that the intellectual foundations of deterrence in Israel were not laid by scholars and thinkers like in the West (by figures such as Bernard Brodie and Herman Kahn in the United States, or Raymond Aron in France) but by practitioners (Ben Gurion and Dayan as well as Shimon Peres and Yigal Allon) who were less keen on developing an in-depth analytical framework.[12]

This dimension of Israeli strategic thinking regarding deterrence leads to a first lesson. Even though deterrence is part, and has always been part, of Israeli strategic culture, it does not fully match the acceptance of the concept in Western military circles. The implications for the case are two-fold. First, as the next section discusses, the Israeli approach of cumulative deterrence induces that the war of 2006 did not render the idea of deterrence vis-à-vis Hezbollah irrelevant, but rather it sees the conflict as a necessary enterprise to maintain status quo on the long-term, or to capitalize "assets in a victory bank," to use Almog's expression. Second, this also means that if deterrence is acknowledged in the Israeli military establishment, it does not imply that the IDF excludes using force in the future against the Party of God, nor would it imply that a new clash would be tantamount to a failure to deter.

In the case of Hezbollah, references to deterrence are rather more difficult to detect in speeches and official documents before 2006. In the first years following the formation of the Party in 1982, the representatives of the Party were using a rhetoric that could not include the idea of deterrence with Israel. Indeed, such concept entails the recognition of the enemy and the resolve to preserve existing status quo. In the 1980s, the ideological platform of Hezbollah would not accommodate with these prerequisites as it was primarily driven by a revolutionary spirit. In the words of Hezbollah's founders such as Abbas Mussawi, Israel was depicted as a Zionist entity that had invaded Lebanon and was occupying large parts of the Southern countryside. As a result, Hezbollah did not acknowledge the very existence of Israel and its political rhetoric was filled by messages of resistance and revolution.

It can be argued that until the mid-1990s, the strategic culture of Hezbollah remained one of a classic militia that relied on suicide attacks against military convoys as its primary tactics. The political thinking within the Party of God in general, and vis-à-vis Israel in particular, evolved dramatically in the aftermath of Lebanon's civil war. In 1992, the accession of Hassan Nasrallah to the position of secretary general following the assassination of Abbas Mussawi was the starting point of a process of Lebanonization that eventually changed both political and military cultures of the organization. The political strategy of Hassan Nasrallah is well known. As Hezbollah became a player in post-civil war Lebanon, the new secretary general balanced revolutionary rhetoric with electoral pragmatism.[13]

The military views of Nasrallah are less documented. In response to Mussawi's assassination on February 16, 1992, Hezbollah fired the first katyusha rockets at Northern Israel. In the days that followed, Nasrallah delivered an interview to Lebanese newspaper, *As Safir*, to discuss this new tactic. The interview can be identified as a turning point in Hezbollah's military strategy vis-à-vis Israel. True the revolutionary message of the 1980s is still palpable:

> The long-term strategy of the Islamic Resistance is clear and does not require additional explanation. It involves fighting against Israel and liberating Jerusalem . . . namely, ending Israel as a state.

But if Nasrallah qualifies this conflict with Israel as an existential one, he also concedes later in the interview:

> We are not unrealistic. We do not pretend that our military capabilities and the numbers of our mujahidin would be enough to regain Jerusalem. . . . We do, however, believe that the resistance has to finish the job it started.[14]

This conclusion of Nasrallah on the military imbalance between his movement and the IDF is a precious one as it paved the way to its strategy for the last 2 decades:

> We have to work instead toward creating a situation in which the enemy is subject to our conditions. We should tell him: 'If you attack us, we will use our katyushas; if you do not attack us, we will not use our katyushas'.[15]

This idea of using rockets as means of coercion was to be put into practice during the clashes of following years, from the April War of 1996 to the July War of 2007.

If these elements constitute the foundations of a potential deterrence strategy of Hezbollah, this latter grew in earnest only after the IDF withdrawal of South Lebanon in 2000. At first, Hezbollah refused to recognize the new border circumscribed by the United Nations (UN) as the so-called "blue line" in Resolution 425. But 2 years later, Nasrallah announced that the organization would respect the demarcation. Meanwhile, Hezbollah made claims concerning the occupied territories of the Shebaa Farms, and only engaged in low-intensity operations against Israel. This led Israeli thinkers to consider that Hezbollah may accept certain rules of the games. In 2004, Daniel Sobelman was optimistically evaluating for the Tel Aviv-based Jaffee Center that "the creation of 'rules of the game' increases the chances that relative quiet will be preserved for a longer period."[16]

One could argue that after 2000, apart from the Shebaa theater, Hezbollah became a status quo force. Only since then, has the rhetoric of deterrence progressively entered into the discourse of Hezbollah's militants and strategists. Today, the shelves of the bookstores in the *Dahya Janoubia* of Beirut are filled with hagiographic books about the movement that detail the military thinking of the Party. This literature, which proliferated after the 2000 Israeli withdrawal, typically looks like propaganda documents masked into phony academic studies. But beyond the bravado that may annoy readers not acquainted with Hezbollah's rhetoric, these documents sometimes contain elements that altogether constitute a coherent body of strategic thought. Hezbollah has indeed produced a vast amount of strategic thinking since the end of the Israeli occupation, either on the strategic values of its missiles or on the practice of psychological warfare.[17] For instance, in his study on Hezbollah's psychological warfare strategy, Lebanese political writer Youssef Nasrallah uses a famous quote from Hassan Nasrallah, who back in 2000 portrayed Israel as "a spider's web" due to its aversion for protracted conflict and explains how this metaphor captures the whole strategy of Hezbollah.[18] There is explicit linkage in the Hezbollah literature between this idea of Israel being a spider's web and its rocket strategy. Specifically the arsenal plays a role which transcends mere warfighting purpose; it is part of a mental bargain with Israel. In other words, it is a tool of deterrence.

As we will see in the next two sections, these developments on both sides about deterrence did not stop after 2006, they actually grew more sophisticated.

THE REMAKING OF ISRAELI MILITARY POSTURE VIS-À-VIS HEZBOLLAH

On the morning of August 14, 2006, a UN-brokered ceasefire put an end to the 33-day war between Israel and Hezbollah. For the first time in its history, Israel ended a conflict without a decisive military result.[19] Following this setback, political and military authorities were confronted with severe criticism, and several investigations were launched to understand the causes of Israel's inability to address the challenge posed by Hezbollah.

The blame was diverse. Some observers were puzzled by the lack of detailed knowledge of intelligence agencies on Hezbollah's military power.[20] In particular, Hezbollah's use of Chinese-made, Iranian-upgraded C-802 radar-guided missiles against an Israeli missile boat patrolling off the Lebanese coast took the planners in Tel Aviv by surprise. Others wondered about the level of military readiness within the IDF to conduct a conventional conflict. But eventually the biggest amount of blame was directed at the supreme command, specifically the failed leadership of both the prime minister and minister of defense in times of crisis.

The first consequence came on August 17 when Minister of Defense Amir Peretz established a military review committee to be led by former Chief of Staff Amnon Lipkin Shahak. But only 5 days after its creation, Peretz's committee was dissolved due to a massive opposition from both the media and the military.

After several other similar attempts in the following weeks, Ehud Olmert decided to appoint a governmental committee of inquiry, which would be responsible for independent investigation on the political and military conduct of the July war. The head of the committee was retired judge Dr. Eliyahu Winograd.

The year was one of critical changes for the Israeli defense apparatus. Political and military leaders in charge during the July war slowly stepped aside. In January, Chief of Staff Lieutenant General Dan Halutz resigned to be replaced by Lieutenant General Gabi Ashkenazi. Later that year, after having lost a vote within the Labor Party, Amir Peretz left the office of defense minister to the new Labor Party, Ehud Barak.

In April, the Winograd committee issued its first interim report, which that confirmed numerous deficiencies in the decisionmaking process. The report argued that Ehud Olmert's decision was not based on "a detailed, comprehensive and authorized military plan, nor based on careful study of the complex characteristics of the Lebanon arena."[21] According to the committee, the period following the IDF's withdrawal from Lebanon in 2000 was characterized as "the era of containment."[22] During that period, Israel restricted its responses to limited strikes on Hezbollah targets and reconnaissance flights over Lebanon. The idea of a fallacious containment approach grew popular among the IDF officers, and pointed to the seemingly lack of Israeli firmness vis-à-vis Hezbollah prior to the 2006 war.[23]

On the question of military readiness, the interim report explained that after the Intifada decade of urban policing mission in Palestinian territories, the IDF was barely prepared to engage in a high-intensity operation that combined airpower and ground forces. For the Winograd Commission, the military leaders:

> did not alert the political decision-makers to the discrepancy between [their] own scenarios and the authorized modes of action, and did not demand — as was necessary under [their] own plans — early mobilization of the reserves so they could be equipped and trained in case a ground operation would be required. ... Even after these facts became known to the political leaders, they failed to adapt the military way of operation and its goals to the reality on the ground.[24]

A month later, the findings of the Winograd report were complemented by the conclusions of the Brodet Commission, a commission mandated to examine the

Israeli defense budget. In its final report, the Brodet Commission argued that a mix of stagnant defense spending, intelligence failures, and ill-suited doctrine and training programs led the IDF to the failure of the Summer 2006 war.

But while the media focused during that period on the mistakes made by the highest echelons of the political-military chain of command, another debate was ensuing among officers and defense thinkers on the evolution of Israeli military thinking and how this was reflected in the pitfalls of 2006. In the aftermath of the war with Hezbollah, a convenient target was the IDF's Operational Theory Research Institute (OTRI) led by Brigadier General Shimon Naveh since its creation in 1995. Dismantled shortly after the war — although the decision had been taken earlier — OTRI became the catalyst of critics of the IDF. An iconoclast inside the military establishment, Naveh had developed a vast project of intellectual transformation within Israel's military establishment that borrowed from postmodern French philosophy, literary theory, architecture and psychology.[25] Some interviewees described the seminars conducted by Naveh as grotesque postgraduate workshops during which philosophers Gilles Deleuze and Felix Guttari were more often quoted than classic military thinkers.[26] Avi Kober reports that during these meetings:

> Naveh was using a diagram resembling a 'square of opposition' that plotted a set of logical relationships between certain propositions referring to military and guerrilla operations. Labeled with phrases such as 'Difference and Repetition — The Dialectics of Structuring and Structure', 'Formless Rival Entities', 'Fractal Maneuver', 'Velocity vs. Rhythms', 'The Wahabi War Machine', 'Postmodern Anarchists' and 'Nomadic Terrorists'.[27]

Three months prior to the 2006 war, a new concept of operations had been issued by OTRI and addressed to the General Staff. According to several insiders, this new concept, titled "General Staff's Operational Art for the IDF," had not undergone proper assimilation processes before its official approval.[28] Its content reflected the heavy influence of American military ideas, and in particular the now-gone concept of effects-based operations which was, back in 2006, a dominant approach inside the IDF, and in particular inside OTRI.[29] In retrospect, military planners denigrated the document. For instance, Major General Gadi Eisenkot, while working in the Joint Staff during the 2006 War, stated that the "manual was a hostile virus in the guise of an operational concept that had infiltrated the military system and made a shambles of it."[30] The numerous attacks against OTRI are not all well founded, in particular the one that links automatically OTRI literature and the IDF performance during the war against Hezbollah. As one officer told us, "The work of OTRI was debatable but it was not the reason why we failed during the July war."[31]

Critics of OTRI's inclination to post-modern thinking were usually coupled with critics of the overreliance of the Joint Staff on airpower, a matter that relates directly to the personality of the Chief of Staff Dan Halutz. A controversial figure, Halutz had contemplated several times in public statements the belief that war could be won solely by airpower. Back in 2001, as the Israeli Air Force Chief, Halutz stated: "Victory is a matter of consciousness. Airpower affects the adversary's consciousness significantly." A year later, he also declared straightforwardly, "Airpower alone can decide, and let alone be the senior partner to such decision."[32] Facing this salvo of incriminating reports, in September 2007 the IDF announced its new 5-year procurement plan named "Tefen 2012" that projected investments of $60 billion, in particular to upgrade ground forces with hundreds of Merkava Mk4 tanks, command and control structures, and unmanned systems.

With the increasing concerns over Iran's nuclear program and the Israeli Air Force (IAF) strike on a Syrian reactor in September 2007, the issue of the Lebanese front, although unsettled, was moved to the background. Discussions and exchanges continued inside the IDF and defense-related think tanks, but after a year and a major institutional crisis, the Israeli political system was moving on. It would take another year before the predicament of Israel's posture vis-à-vis Hezbollah resurfaced in the media. On October 3, 2008, Major General Gadi Eisenkot, then Israeli Northern Commander, accepted an interview with the newspaper, *Yedioth Ahronoth*, to discuss the current state of security in Northern Israel. When asked about the likelihood of a new conflict against Hezbollah, Eisenkot straightforwardly declared that:

> What happened in the Dahya quarter in Beirut in 2006 will happen in every village from which Israel is fired on. We will apply disproportionate force on it and cause great damage and destruction there.

He went on to say, "From our standpoint, these are not civilian villages, they are military bases." Leaving no space for ambiguity, Eisenkot added "This is not a recommendation. This is a plan. And it has been approved."[33]

Dahya (Arabic for "suburbs") commonly designates the name of a densely populated group of Shia neighborhoods in southern Beirut where Hezbollah's headquarters are located.[34] During the first days of the 2006 war, it was the target of massive air strikes by the IAF. In the weeks following Eisenkot's remarks, intense speculations grew in both Israeli and foreign media regarding the implementation by the IDF of a warfighting posture that would derive from the *Dahya* strategy inspired by Eisenkot's interview and whether that might trigger a new conflict with Hezbollah. In fact, the debate was mainly based on a set of military ideas promoted by three close thinkers: Gadi Eisenkot, the Major General who headed the Military Operations Directorate of the General Staff when the 2006 war broke out; Gabi Siboni, a retired IDF colonel and a research fellow from Israel's Institute for National Security Studies (INSS) and who commanded the Golani Brigade just as Eisenkot and both are said to be "close friends;"[35] and Giora Eiland, a retired Major General and former National Security Advisor who left this position in June 2006 to become a research fellow at the INSS as well.

A few days after Eisenkot's interview, Gabi Siboni, published an article on the INSS website titled "Disproportionate Force: Israel's Concept of Response in Light of the Second Lebanon War." Similarly to Eisenkot's statement, Siboni explained that, "With an outbreak of hostilities, the IDF will need to act immediately, decisively, and with force that is disproportionate to the enemy's actions and the threat it poses."[36] Furthermore, 1 month after Siboni's and Eisenkot's arguments, Giora Eiland explored the very same ideas in an article of the INSS in-house journal, *Strategic Assessment*:

There is one way to prevent the Third Lebanon War and win it if it does break out . . . to make it clear to Lebanon's allies and through them to the Lebanese government and people that the next war will be between Israel and Lebanon and not between Israel and Hezbollah. Such a war will lead to the elimination of the Lebanese military, the destruction of the national infrastructure, and intense suffering among the population. There will be no recurrence of the situation where Beirut residents (not including the Dahya quarter) go to the beach and cafes while Haifa residents sit in bomb shelters.[37]

Despite journalistic speculations, Siboni, Eisenkot, and Eiland did not pretend to represent a particular school of military thought. In fact, their views were reminiscent of past Israeli statements on the use of force as viewed in the previous chapter. Still, the speculations on the *Dahya* strategy were exacerbated further after the IDF conducted Operation CAST LEAD against Hamas in the Gaza Strip from December 27, 2008, to January 18, 2009. This major operation aimed at putting an end to the rocket attacks conducted either by Hamas or militias in the Gaza Strip. The first phase started with an air campaign relying on F-16 fighter jets and AH-64 *Apache* attack helicopters that targeted homes of Palestinian militiamen and command posts, but it also led to the destruction of public infrastructures. It was then followed by a ground invasion, Israeli tanks and troops seizing control of large parts of the Palestinian territory.

The operation triggered a major international controversy. In late-2009, the UN formed a mission conducting an investigation into the 2009 Gaza conflict between the IDF and the Palestinian organization,

Hamas. While looking in retrospect at the Eisenkot's statements, as well as at Siboni and Eiland's writings, the UN mission concluded that the *Dahya* strategy had indeed been applied in the Gaza Strip. The much-discussed report of the UN Fact Finding Mission on the Gaza Conflict (popularly referenced as the Goldstone Report in the name of the head of the UN Mission) extensively quotes Eisenkot's interview to affirm that:

> the mission does not have to consider whether Israeli military officials were directly influenced by these writings. It is able to conclude from a review of the facts on the ground that it witnessed for itself that what is prescribed as the best strategy appears to have been precisely what was put into practice.[38]

To this day, IDF officials strictly deny any linkage between Eisenkot's ideas and the conduct of Operation CAST LEAD. Some officers underline that the *Dahya* strategy is tailored for Israel's conflict with Hezbollah, not with Hamas. Others downplay the relevance of the so-called strategy as "a mere topic constructed by the media."[39] When asked, Gabi Siboni answered that "This is no more than folkore, *Dahya* is a concept, nothing more."[40] The truth lies in between. It may be misleading at operational level to believe the 2008 war in the Gaza Strip was the application of a military doctrine born of the confrontation with Hezbollah 2 years before. Still, the response of the IDF to the Palestinian groups surely restored and reemphasized its resolve and credibility. In that perspective, it could be seen as an indirect way to enforce deterrence on the northern front.

This constitutes no revolution as it relates clearly to Israel's traditional strategic culture and deterrence thinking. The real novelty is that this Israeli calculus of deterrence, historically designed against the Arab militaries, was now considered to be relevant in front of Hezbollah. This change in Israel's military posture vis-à-vis Hezbollah is based on two major conclusions drawn from the 2006 war. First, the air strikes against Hezbollah's headquarters in the first days were considered to be effective. Their scale took Secretary General Nasrallah and his inner circle by surprise, but moreover they severely weakened the command and control structure of Hezbollah's military body. This statement contradicts explicitly the popular narrative that aerial bombardments did not work, and that the IDF's failures were, in fact, caused by their overreliance on this instrument of military power.[41] On the contrary, the advocates of the *Dahya* concept argue that these strikes were effective, but were not leveraged at the political level due to unclear objectives. Furthermore, the tense debates between Israel's prime minister office and the U.S. State Department on the need to avoid targeting Lebanese infrastructures had blurred Israel's resolve.

For the proponents of the *Dahya* concept, this leads to the second conclusion. The distinction between Lebanese authorities and Hezbollah was allegedly counterproductive because of the U.S. diplomatic call to Israel for restraint concerning Lebanese targets that impeded the IDF's ability to coerce the Party of God. Eiland's, Siboni's, and Eisenkot's statements are explicit. The air strikes should indistinctly be extended to Lebanese infrastructures. This reasoning takes into account Hezbollah's increased influence within the Lebanese State since the conflict of 2006. Following the June 2009 elections, Hezbollah held 13 seats in the 128-member Lebanese Parliament and two in the cabinet. Moreover, in a December 2009 vote, the

Lebanese Parliament allowed Hezbollah to retain its arsenal of weapons. Furthermore, the Israelis carefully observed the violent clashes between Hezbollah and Sunni Lebanese factions in Beirut in the Spring of 2008. For some Israeli thinkers, such clashes suggested that a devastating Israeli retaliation on national facilities could turn the population against the Party.

The lessons from Israel's intelligence failures prior to the 2006 conflict, and in particular the realization of the vast rocket and missile arsenal Hezbollah was now controlling, is at the core of the *Dahya* concept. Isreal also realizes that it cannot militarily destroy the entire arsenal. It can degrade its scale, it can prevent some flow of weapons coming from Iran and Syria, but eventually it has to cope with it and accept a certain degree of vulnerability. Following his interview with *Yedioth Ahronoth*, Eisenkot explained this phenomenon in a subsequent article written in 2010 for INSS (Siboni's and Eiland's research center) titled "A Changed Threat? The Response on the Northern Arena." For Eisenkot, Israeli planners face an evolving environment where the traditional scenario of a surprise attack on Israel's territory is shifting to "the new reality that includes extensive rockets and missile fire at Israeli population centers together with the use of terrorism and guerrilla tactics."[42] In fact, Eisenkot was already underlining this challenge in a research paper written in 1997 for the U.S. Army. "As Israel's neighbours begin to acquire long range missiles, the strategic balance in the region will shift, and Israel will be required to adapt its strategic posture."[43]

Eiland also emphasizes the fact that:

> the number of long and medium range rockets within the overall arsenal skyrocketed, which will enable Hezbollah to continue firing even if Israel occupies the entire area between the border and the Litani River.[44]

Siboni portrays this shift as the new strategic concept of Israel's enemies:

> The size of Israel and the fact that it has no strategic depth made Israel's enemies assume that high trajectory fire aimed at the Israeli home front in large quantities and with a minimum of variables would allow them to achieve their goal.[45]

The proliferation of these vectors, in particular those possessed by Hezbollah, upsets Israeli historical efforts to protect its territory at all costs. Since the late-1940s, Israel's strategic culture has been shaped by constraints such as its absence of strategic depth and its limited manpower, leaving the country at the mercy of protracted conflicts that could endanger its very existence. To bypass these elements, Israeli leaders opted for offensive doctrines enabling the launching of preemptive campaigns that would swiftly move the battles to enemy territory. For Arab states such as Egypt and Syria, ballistic missiles proved the perfect instrument to circumvent Israel's military dominance. Missiles disrupt classic air power and constitute a major challenge to homeland defense.

This is why the evolving thinking of Israel vis-à-vis Hezbollah also relates to Israel's experience with missile defenses which are becoming a key feature of its military posture against such groups. For the Israeli policymakers, the first wake-up call with regards to the missile threat came with the war of the cities between Iran and Iraq in 1988, during which Saddam Hussein used Scud missile strikes against Tehran as a new weapon of coercion. At first, the political class in Jerusalem justified development of missile defense in the name of pragmatism and opportunism. Israeli politicians became aware that the security — or the sanctuarization — of their territory had come to be jeopardized by increasing regional proliferation. It was also an opportunistic move, because Israel was taking advantage of the early impetus in Ronald Reagan's Strategic Defense Initiative. Within this cooperation framework, the burden of developing the systems was mostly taken on by the United States.

The second and crucial game changer was the 2006 war. The ability of Hezbollah to reach Israel urban sites even during the last days of the war evidenced for Israeli planners the necessity to reconsider their traditional neglect of defensive means. The result was the building of the Israeli-made system, Iron Dome.

Missile defense has become a precious tool for the Israeli government. It reassures citizens of their safety and mitigates the psychological effects of missile warfare. But because of the various systems developed or under development in Israel, there is widespread confusion over the exact level of readiness and coverage of its missile defense architecture. Given the current passion of Israeli politicians for these systems, party leaders and government officials maintain a kind of ambiguity regarding the ultimate objective of missile defense and frequently imply that these systems aim at defending the homeland as a whole. In reality, what the existing systems protect is, first and foremost, critical infrastructure and military bases. Major General Eisenkot, Deputy Chief of Staff of the IDF, triggered a public controversy during a speech at the University of Haifa in 2010 when he stated:

> The residents of Israel shouldn't be under the illusion that someone will open an umbrella over their heads. . . the systems are designed to protect military bases, even if this means that citizens suffer discomfort during the first days of battle.[46]

It is the essential reason why missile defense efforts, and in particular the recent successes of Iron Dome,[47] do not translate into a rebalancing between offensive and defensive tenets for the Israeli military. In the case of Israel-Hezbollah competition, they complement the deterrence posture as reflected by the *Dahya* debate, but they certainly do not constitute the sole answer.

This is also the reason why the IDF recently built a new corps named the Depth Corps, a special unit to coordinate and conduct clandestine operations in enemy territory against missile- and rocket-launcher sites. This new corps reflects the continuing will of the IDF to retain the option of preemptive strikes.[48]

In a nutshell, the scenario that drives Israel's contemporary military thinking regarding its northern front can be imagined as beginning with a provocation from Hezbollah, such as abducting Israeli soldiers or launching rockets on civilian areas of northern Israel. Then Israel responds with massive IAF air strikes on Beirut and southern Lebanon combined with a small contingent of forward ground forces operating in Lebanon to destroy rocket-launching sites, and missile defense systems on alert to intercept projectiles. This combination is expected to lead to a rapid coercion of the Party of God. The issue with this thinking is that, as for many deterrence doctrines, Israeli posture posits an exclusive bilateral competition with

Hezbollah. This prerequisite is essential for the stability of the deterrence approach, but it means that any exogenous change impacting the competition is likely to jeopardize the calculus. As we will see in the last section, such game changers do exist.

HEZBOLLAH'S LESSONS

For Hezbollah, the 2006 war resembled less a catastrophic failure than a well-timed opportunity to restore its image as freedom fighters 6 years after Israel's withdrawal from South Lebanon and to regain political leverage inside Lebanon a year after the Syrian military left the country. Whereas Hezbollah looked isolated in the spring of 2006, it would exit the war in August galvanized.[49] Despite the very fact that its military structures, either in the South or in Beirut, were destroyed by the Israeli air strikes and that its manpower had been likewise reduced following the battle with Israeli ground forces, Hezbollah made all efforts at the end of the war to paint itself as the victorious one.[50]

In retrospect, Nasrallah turned an ill-conceived provocation against Israel into a demonstration of Hezbollah's power to coerce the Zionist entity, and an illustration that the Party of God was the ultimate defender of the Arab cause in the region. In this 34-day war, the endurance of Hezbollah vis-à-vis the powerful Israeli forces took Arab rulers by surprise. At first, many of the latter condemned Hezbollah's aggression at the Israel-Lebanon border as an irresponsible act that triggered the war. But the intensity and the scale of Israel's reaction, coupled with the ability of the Lebanese organization to continue defying the IDF, changed the mind-set of Arab public opinion in such a way that Arab leaders in Beirut, Cairo, and in Gulf capitals revised their initial condemnation. Hezbollah's military performance was an embarrassment for many old Arab rulers because it indirectly underlined the failure of Arab conventional armies which have never achieved this level of resistance against Israel. A previous study conducted for the U.S. Army War College evidenced this reality:

> Hezbollah inflicted more Israeli casualties per Arab fighter in 2006 than did any of Israel's state opponents in the 1956, 1967, 1973, or 1982 Arab-Israeli interstate wars. Hezbollah's skills in conventional warfighting were clearly imperfect in 2006—but they were also well within the observed bounds of other state military actors in the Middle East and elsewhere, and significantly superior to many such states.[51]

As a result, the first objective Hezbollah needed to obtain by September 2006 was obvious: to convert the military capital it acquired through the war into political capital. In the weeks prior to the July war, Hezbollah was under severe pressure because of the battle between Lebanon's pro- and anti-Syria political blocs that had been triggered by the 2005 assassination of Rafic Hariri, the former prime minister and opponent to Syrian military occupation. Suddenly, after the end of the conflict, Hezbollah's political latitude vis-à-vis the government of Fouad Siniora was greatly expanded.

In a speech given a month later, Nasrallah stated that "Tears don't protect anyone," an explicit reference to Siniora, who wept several times in official speeches during the July war. Nasrallah went on, "No army in the world will be able to make us drop the weapons from our hands." In the same speech, Nasrallah described the war as "a divine, historic and strategic victory."[52] Since then, the expression of "divine victory" became the authoritative expression to depict the conflict in all Hezbollah's official literature.[53]

The narrative conveyed in Hezbollah's literature and public declarations balanced between sacred references and nationalistic claims in order to preempt critics at political level on the risks endured by Lebanon because of its agenda. As a result, the 2006 war quickly became part of the mythology of the Party, inspiring numerous urban legends about fighters that bravely defeated the Israelis in the fights of the South Lebanon villages.[54] But beyond the making of such glorious and quasi-mythological narratives, the leadership of Hezbollah was fully aware that, to preserve its political gains on the long haul, it had not only to rearm but also to reassess its military strategy.

Various sources suggest that in the same way that the IDF implemented a thorough process of lessons learned after the July War, Hezbollah, along with the Iranian Revolutionary Guards, conducted their own comprehensive after-action review.[55] But whereas Israel's political and military establishment underwent a bottom-up rethinking of its strategy, for Hezbollah, the 2006 war confirmed that its increasing reliance on rocket and missile warfare had been the best strategic option taken by the organization to circumvent Israeli military power. Hezbollah's rockets flying over Haifa and other cities awed the Israeli public and produced a sentiment of high vulnerability among the population. For Hezbollah, this meant that its arsenal could compel Israeli governments to yield in the future. However, aside from the declaratory bravado of Nasrallah, the war was surely not a military victory: the massive destruction of its headquarters in the suburbs of Beirut and South Lebanon severely disrupted the chain of command of operations and evidenced obvious loopholes in the air defense capabilities of the Party.

In the years following the 2006 conflict, Hezbollah therefore focused on this revised strategic calculus: to invest in rockets and missiles with improved range and accuracy, while acquiring air defense systems. The logic was to strengthen the resolve of the Party to strike Israel deep inside its territory and to enhance the ability of Hezbollah to mitigate, or at least absorb, the impact of an Israeli bombing campaign through defensive means.

Today, the number of rockets and missiles under the control of Hezbollah is difficult to know. In September 2008, Israeli Minister of Defense Ehud Barak estimated that they counted 40,000 rockets. One year later, President Shimon Peres suggested that the figure was close to 80,000.[56] IDF officials interviewed for our research stated that the number was approximately 42,000 rockets plus 4,000 short- to mid-range missiles.[57]

The quality of the arsenal dramatically improved as Hezbollah acquired rockets using guidance systems and with extended range. During that same period, the arms race crossed a new threshold as Hezbollah started acquiring ballistic missiles. It is believed that, through Syria, the Party acquired M-600 short-range ballistic missiles, a variant of the Fateh-110, which can carry a 1,100-pound warhead and has a range of 210 kilometers (km).[58] According to weapon engineers, the inertial guidance system of the M-600 enables the missile to strike within 500 yards of a target at maximum range.

In the months that followed the July War, Israel expressed numerous threats of retaliation and stressed red lines regarding the new build-up conducted by Hezbollah. As the war was still vivid in Israeli memories, the Israeli Joint Staff may have feared that Hezbollah would rapidly rearm. It may have feared that Hezbollah, being emboldened by the last round, would dare to trigger a new confrontation. Only a month after the ceasefire, Nasrallah was indeed declaring "Today, 22 September, 2006, the resistance is stronger than any time since 1982."[59] Nasrallah's statement was not grounded in operational realities, but reflected the bolstered behavior of Hezbollah in the post-war period. In the following months, Israeli authorities repeatedly made the case to their Western counterparts that Hezbollah was acquiring capabilities that challenged the post-cease fire status quo. But still the IDF showed restraint.

To conduct the rearmament of Hezbollah, cooperation with Syria and Iran proved even more crucial than prior to the 2006 war. In the first months that followed the war, the man at the center of this cooperative effort was Imad Mughniyeh, an historical figure of Hezbollah's military branch whose reputation as one of the most wanted terrorists in the world had reached a quasi-mystical level among terrorism experts. According to the Lebanese newspaper, *Al-Akhbar*, Mughniyeh had been put in charge of the post-2006 buildup, an effort that he conducted in coordination with his inner contacts in Syria and Iran.[60] Mughniyeh did so until the evening of February 12, 2008, when he was killed when his car exploded in the Kfar Sousa neighborhood of Damascus. Details of this operation are still lacking, but it inflicted a severe blow to Hezbollah. Although one needs to remain cautious on the conjectures that surround any discussion of Mughniyeh, the location of his assassination, Damascus, revealed the close cooperation between Syria, Iran, and Hezbollah in the aftermath of the 2006 war.

In the case of Syria, this reinvigorated cooperation was the result of the new approach taken by President Bashar al-Assad vis-à-vis Hezbollah. In the years following Bashar's rise to power Nasrallah became a regular visitor to Damascus, and the new Syrian president did not hesitate to be seen publicly with him. The Syrian regime cast aside the elder Assad's restraint and developed the idea of an anti-imperialist axis represented by Syria, Hezbollah, and Iran. As a sign of this evolution, during the 2006 summer war between Israel and Hezbollah, the streets of Damascus and Homs were littered with flyers proclaiming the glory of the movement, and Nasrallah in particular.

On top of this political support, Syria has lent considerable logistical support to the Party of God's military structure, particularly by maintaining the supply corridors used by Iran to supply missiles and other arms to Hezbollah. If Hezbollah's current missile strike force constitutes a real tool of dissuasion to the Jewish state rather than a simple nuisance to northern Israel, it is largely thanks to Bashar al-Assad's Syrian regime. This was explicitly acknowledged by Nasrallah in 2012 during a speech he gave on the 6th anniversary of the July War:

> Syria is a path for the Resistance and a bridge of communication between the Resistance and Iran. . . . I have two [proofs] for Syria's role [in supporting the Resistance]. The first one is that the most important rockets that targeted Haifa and the center of 'Israel' were made by Syrian military and given to the Resistance. Syria was an aid to the Resistance and gave weapons that we used in the July War.[61]

On numerous occasions, these transfers led American officials to incriminate the Syrian authorities. In February 2009, U.S. Director for National Intelligence Dennis Blair stated explicitly that "Syrian military support to Hezbollah has increased substantially over the past 5 years, especially since the 2006 Israel-Hezbollah war." A year later, in testimony before the House Foreign Affairs Committee, Assistant Secretary of State for Near Eastern Affairs Ambassador Jeffrey Feltman declared that "the Syrian Army's 2005 withdrawal from Lebanon and Hezbollah's 2006 conflict with Israel deepened the strategic interdependence between the Syrian state and Hezbollah."[62]

During that same period, Syria was accused of transferring Scud-D ballistic missiles to Hezbollah. With a range of 700-km, Scud-D missiles could reach either Jerusalem or Tel Aviv. Although Syrian authorities denied the charges, the U.S. State Department issued a statement, saying:

> the United States condemns in the strongest terms the transfer of any arms, and especially ballistic missile systems such as the Scud, from Syria to Hezbollah. . . . The transfer of these arms can only have a destabilizing effect on the region, and would pose an immediate threat to both the security of Israel and the sovereignty of Lebanon.[63]

This transfer followed a first allegation that the Syrian regime had provided Hezbollah with M-600 missiles. There have been also rumors that Syria had provided Hezbollah with surface-to-air missile systems including the SA-2, SA-8, and the SA-24. The two last ones are mobile systems, easy to conceal, and would represent key assets for air defense if Israel was to launch a bombing campaign.[64] In addition, Hezbollah's men are said to have been sent to Syria for training on the SA-8 system. Likewise, Nicholas Blanford and Bilal Saab reported that "Hezbollah may also have acquired the Misagh-2 shoulder fired missile produced in Iran and based on Chinese technology."[65] This man-portable low- to very-low-altitude surface-to-air missile would prove crucial if Hezbollah fighters were under air attacks from the IDF.

All these developments reflected the coherent re-action of Hezbollah following its strategic review of the July War, in particular the lesson that improved air defense systems were crucially needed. A month later, Brigadier General Yossi Baidatz, the Intelligence Research Director of the IDF, stated before the Israeli Knesset:

> Hezbollah has an arsenal of thousands of rockets of all types and ranges, including long-range solid-fuel rockets and more precise rockets. . . . The long-range missiles in Hezbollah's possession enable them to fix their launch areas deep inside Lebanon, and they cover longer, larger ranges than what we have come across in the past. Hezbollah of 2006 is different from Hezbollah of 2010 in terms its military capabilities, which have developed significantly.[66]

Baidatz went on to underline the change of patterns in the Hezbollah-Syria-Iran cooperation framework:

> Weapons are transferred to Hezbollah on a regular basis and this transfer is organized by the Syrian and Iranian regimes. Therefore, it should not be called smuggling of arms to Lebanon—it is organized and official transfer.[67]

But if Hezbollah increased and improved its arsenal, it also adapted to two new developments: the deployment of the UN Interim Force in Lebanon (UNIFIL) forces in South Lebanon and the new efforts of Israeli forces to detect its launcher sites. Following the July war, the UN Security Council decided that the UNIFIL forces, initially created in 1978 in the midst of Israel's intervention in Lebanon, would be now deployed in the South to enforce the ceasefire concluded in August 2006. Initially UNIFIL was to be staffed with 15,000 soldiers, but contributing nations never provided more than 13,000 men. Obviously, such a mission should have challenged Hezbollah's power in South Lebanon, its historical stronghold. In reality, UNIFIL had to cope with Hezbollah, rather than the other way around. As a French official in the Ministry of Defense reminded, "UNIFIL heavily relies on cooperation with Hezbollah, there is no way it could perform its mission without this form of tacit coexistence."[68] For several years, the arrangements UNIFIL had to make in some of the South Lebanon villages where Hezbollah rules have been documented. Additionally, UNIFIL officers were fully aware of Hezbollah's military build-up in the area, a *fait accompli* that contravenes the idea of UN Resolution 1701 to establish "between the Blue Line and the Litani river of an area free of any armed personnel, assets and weapons other than those of the Government of Lebanon and of UNIFIL deployed in this area."[69] Still, pragmatism prevailed, and there was an implicit division of labor which allowed UNIFIL forces to monitor certain areas while letting Hezbollah maintain its hold in others.

Meanwhile, Israel's new emphasis on intelligence to detect and destroy Hezbollah's launcher sites urged the Party to rethink the location of these sites. As a result, Hezbollah is said to have moved them further north in the countryside. In March 2011, the IDF leaked to the *Washington Post* a map that showed 1,000 bunkers, hidden weapons storage facilities, and surveillance sites spread all around Lebanon, whether in the north or in the Bekaa valley.

DUE TO COPYRIGHT RESTRICTIONS
SOME OR ALL IMAGES ARE NOT INCLUDED

Source: "Israeli military maps Hezbollah bunkers,"*Washington Post*.[70]

Map 1. Hezbollah Underground Infrastructure in South Lebanon.

This repositioning of Hezbollah's sites has several consequences. First, it deemphasizes the place of South Lebanon as the center of gravity for a future conflict. Second, it underlines the growing range of the Party's arsenal if that arsenal can be stationed far away from the Israel-Lebanon border. Overall, this means that a new confrontation would look more like an air war than a long and massive war in the Southern villages.

This obviously relates to Israel's own evolution with the *Dahya* debate discussed earlier in this monograph. Since 2006, strategic stability between Israel and Hezbollah has not only been reached by the new balance of forces that prevailed but also by indirect dialogue. This dialogue does not equal concrete back-channel meetings but rather ostentatious public communication on both sides to convey its message to the other, the result being that each competitor better knows the culture and mind-set of the other. In the case of Hezbollah, this understanding of Israel should not be underestimated. It transpires from the multiple statements made by Hassan Nasrallah and other leaders of the Party. Indeed, Hezbollah's strategists seem to have a fine comprehension of Israel's evolving military posture, but furthermore they have been discussing Israeli strategy at length through public speeches or propaganda books. On numerous occasions since the July War, Nasrallah detailed his vision of the Party's arsenal as a deterrent against the IDF new build-up. In the last years, one of the best-selling DVDs of Nasrallah's speeches in Lebanon is the so-called *Khitaab al radaa'* (Speech of the deterrence). In this 1-hour speech, Nasrallah talks directly to the IDF saying:

> They think they can demolish Dahya's buildings as we barely 'puncture their walls'. But I tell them today: You destroy a Dahya building and we will destroy buildings in Tel Aviv. . . . If you target Beirut's Rafik Hariri International Airport, we will strike Tel Aviv's Ben Gurion International Airport. If you target our electricity stations, we will target yours. If you target our plants, we will target yours.[71]

Some parts of the video are used in the inaugural documentary that is aired at the entrance of the

Mleeta Resistance Museum built by Hezbollah in the South after the 2006 war. The Museum itself is filled with messages of deterrence such as maps of Israeli locations in the range of Hezbollah's missiles. (See Figure 1.)

Figure 1. Propaganda Poster in the Mleeta Museum, "If you strike . . . we will strike."[72]

In fact, the more Israel was discussing the *Dahya* concept, the more Hassan Nasrallah insisted on Hezbollah's abilities to retaliate. In May 2010, he was again talking to the Israeli decisionmakers, saying in a public speech:

> If you blockade our coastline, shores and ports, all mil-
> itary and commercial ships heading toward Palestine
> throughout the Mediterranean Sea will be targeted by
> the rockets of the Islamic Resistance.[73]

A year later, he threatened an invasion of the Galilee if Israel was to launch a new war on Lebanon:

> I'm telling the fighters of the Islamic resistance: Be
> ready for the day, should war be forced upon Leba-
> non, where the resistance's leadership will ask you to
> take over the Galilee.[74]

For Hezbollah, such deterrence rhetoric is a dou-ble-edge sword. It shapes implicit and explicit redlines for escalation and therefore it dissipates uncertainties vis-à-vis Israel on the likelihood of a new conflict. But through that process, Hezbollah must indirectly rec-ognize its adversary as a political entity. So, in return, the revolutionary design of the Party fades away, and it becomes a defensive and status-quo centered political force.

Scholarship in security studies shows that deter-rence remains a stable system as long as each of the competitors maintains a robust chain of command which strictly controls its means of deterrence.[75] How-ever, Hezbollah has never been an autonomous actor which indigenously built its deterrent. It relied and still relies substantially on the regimes in Syria and Iran. Moreover, even though the Party remains the biggest security actor in Lebanon, it does not specifi-cally control its territory. In fact, the most interesting paradox may be that the more Hezbollah becomes a military power able to deter Israel, the more it de-pends on external actors and the more it puts the do-mestic stability in Lebanon at risk.

The spreading of Hezbollah's military posts deep inside the country changes the internal equation between the Party and the Lebanese forces. More precisely, it exacerbates the ascendant of the former on the latter. It gives even more relevance to the Israeli calculus to consider the Lebanese government to be responsible for Hezbollah's operations against Israel. This also reveals the fundamental caveat in the deterrence game between Hezbollah and Israel. The very fact that even though Hezbollah is a well-structured, well-trained military organization, it still remains a nonstate actor competing with regular forces on the same territory.

It is widely known in Beirut and elsewhere that there is a tacit agreement between Hezbollah and Lebanese armed forces over the control of the national territory. As a result, order and security in the southern region as well as Southern Beirut are provided by Hezbollah. But at political level, the deterrence calculus vis-à-vis Israel also reads as a convenient way for Hezbollah to sell the rationale for maintaining its hold on its arsenal and avoiding any disarmament inside Lebanon. In a way, one could argue that the current deterrence rhetoric that emerged in Hezbollah's statements since the 2000s replaced the resistance rhetoric. Even though this latter is still present, the movement transformed itself into a defensive organization rather than a revolutionary one. This subtle change was coined by some pundits close to Hezbollah, "Resistance in defensive mode." Months after the July War, Deputy Secretary General of the Party Sheikh Naim Qasim acknowledged this evolution:

> Our objective is not to wage a conventional war, nor to maintain positions or carry weapons for public show.

> Our aim is to have the capability to defend, in the event of an aggression.

He goes on, "As long as Israel remains aggressive in the region, we must fear this aggression. These arms will then remain to confront and defend against aggression."[76]

To understand the domestic dimension of the uses of a deterrence rhetoric vis-à-vis Israel, one has to be mindful of the pressures facing Hezbollah since 2006. In fact, the 2006 War put a momentary hold on the long struggle between pro-Syrian and anti-Syrian forces in Lebanon. But less than 2 years later, hostilities started again. In May 2008, the government decided to reassign the commander of security at Beirut International Airport, Brigadier General Wafiq Shuqeir, to the Army Command as he was suspected of working closely with Hezbollah. Additionally, the Lebanese government declared Hezbollah's telecommunications network illegal, calling it "a threat to state security."[77] In response to this challenge, Hezbollah took to the streets and led an operation to take over West Beirut (mainly the Sunni neighborhood). In less than 12 hours, Hezbollah-affiliated militias were outnumbering police and military forces.[78] After more than a week, pro-government and opposition factions agreed to cease the hostilities and to revoke the initial decisions. Since then, the military power of Hezbollah has not been challenged again, but the 2008 episode is an enduring illustration of the long struggle inside Lebanon between the Party and its Sunni rivals that could be reignited in the coming years. The paradox here is Israel's interest on this issue. Over the long term, Israel prefers a marginalized and weak Hezbollah, but on the short term, a strong Hezbollah in Beirut means that command and control of its arsenal is secured, and decisionmaking is more or less predictable.

All in all, the development of a deterrence bargain in the Israel-Hezbollah competition following the 2006 war should be neither underestimated nor overestimated. Stability has prevailed in the area because of effective strategies on both sides to negate the edge of the other. Hezbollah increased its offensive capabilities such as missiles and rockets, while building a better air defense coverage. Meanwhile, Israel renovated its military position by relying on a deterrence posture that mixes elements of punishment (the *Dahya* concept) and denial (the rise of its missile defense systems). The bargain has proved effective, at least for the last 7 years. But as we emphasized at the beginning of this monograph, deterrence is a social construct that is neither natural nor eternal. This is why it is also important to identify what could test and maybe disrupt the deterrence stability between Israel and Hezbollah.

GAME CHANGERS IN THE DETERRENCE SYSTEM

Faith in the stability of deterrence can sometimes be driven by a retroactive illusion. It can inadvertently neglect the critical rules and processes that are necessary to sustain this stability in the long term. As we argued in the first section, a deterrence situation such as the Israel-Hezbollah stand-off since 2006 is a social construct emanating from strategic players. It is not a natural state and requires constant adaptations to mitigate the risks of miscalculation. This is why some scholars of deterrence have argued that, paradoxically, we only know in retrospect if deterrence was working when a deterrence situation ends (e.g., the collapse of the Union of Soviet Socialist Republics [USSR]), or fails (Israel-Arab wars).[79]

At the time of this writing, strategic stability between Israel and Hezbollah prevails because of the mutual understanding that this remains the best outcome of their competition. However, this principle only works as long as this competition is not altered by external factors. This is why we need to be mindful of the potential tests to the Israel-Hezbollah deterrence equation. In this last section, we look at three major issues that may constitute such tests: the development of the Syrian crisis, the Iranian nuclear issue, and the evolution of Lebanese politics.

Opening the Syrian Front.

The Syrian crisis started in March 2011 in the midst of uprisings in other Arab countries. Following the first demonstrations in rural areas such as Deraa or Deir el Zhor, the government of Bashar al-Assad reacted with a combination of timid pledges of reforms and brutal repression. On a general basis, the fall of Assad's regime would represent a severe loss, both politically and militarily, for Hezbollah. As explained in the previous chapter, the Party benefited from Bashar al-Assad which made Syria not only a zone of transit for Iranian supplies to South Lebanon, but a strategic partner that trained Hezbollah militants in several domains, including air defense systems. This explains why the leadership of the movement feels it owes a strategic debt to Damascus.

During the first months, Hezbollah's rulers preserved their traditional posture by offering full support to the Syrian regime. Many of the speeches given by the Hezbollah secretary general concerning Syria denounced the predatory strategies of external powers (namely the United States and Israel) directed at the Syrian regime and increasingly diverted the attention of his audiences to the seemingly more urgent Palestinian cause. In other words, the movement developed a narrative of the crisis which was identical to that presented by the government of Bashar al-Assad. Meanwhile, the movement consistently denied all implications stemming from certain media coverage, notably emanating from the opposition Free Syrian Army or Israeli sources, which has conjured up charges of Hezbollah's role as a logistical and military supporter of the Syrian repression.

Things changed radically in the summer of 2012, and more precisely after the July 18 bomb attack in Damascus that killed several key officials of the Syrian security apparatus (among them Syrian Defense Minister Dawoud Rajiha and Deputy Defense Minister Assef Shawkat). The attack occurred the same day Nasrallah was scheduled to deliver a speech to celebrate the 6th anniversary of the victory against Israel. In his final speech, Nasrallah chose not to circumvent the Syrian issue, but to embrace Assad's fight, praising the role of Syrian leader in Hezbollah's fight against Israel and naming Assef Shawkat a martyr that helped the Party's acquisition of rockets that were launched on Israel during the 2006 war.[80]

Following the attack of July 2012, the Syrian regime entered a new threshold in the escalation process and has resorted to extensive and indiscriminate use of airpower over the major disputed urban centers like Aleppo and Homs. In addition, there has been an increasing involvement of Syria's allies, Iran and Hezbollah, on the battlefield. During August and September 2012, hundreds of Iranian Revolutionary Guards were deployed in Damascus to offer expertise such as psychological warfare and monitoring of social networks.[81]

With regards to Hezbollah, there have been since the beginning of the revolution repeated cases of clashes between its fighters and the Free Syrian Army (FSA) in villages near the Syria-Lebanon border. But, as the regime in Damascus faces crucial scarcity of manpower due to desertion or defection, Hezbollah and Iranian Pasdarans train pro-Assad militias such as the Chabihas and Jeish al Chaa'bi to replace the conventional forces in several parts of the country.

Conflict involving Hezbollah's fighters intensified in the Lebanon-Syria border area, close to Homs. In August 2012, Lebanese media revealed the death of Musa Ali Shahimi, a commander of Hezbollah's military branch in this area. The circumstances of the death were not clear, but in September, Ali Nassif, another commander, died under the same conditions. According to a declaration from the Free Syrian Army, Nassif died in clashes in the town of Qusair. In this same town, the Free Syrian Army allegedly captured a dozen of Hezbollah's fighters.

Things got worse in the following months as Hezbollah raised the level of its cooperation with Assad's forces. This reached a new threshold in the so-called Qusair battle in the spring of 2013, during which the Party of God openly fought on the Syrian soil against the rebels. In late-May, Hassan Nasrallah publicly acknowledged this involvement during one of his speeches commemorating the 13th anniversary of Israel's withdrawal from South Lebanon. He asserted:

> Where we need to be, we will be. Where we began to assume our responsibilities, we will continue to as-

sume our responsibilities. To defeat this very, very dangerous conspiracy [against Syria] we will bear any sacrifices and all the consequences.[82]

As Hezbollah's calculus evolved during the Syrian crisis, so did the Israeli's. At first, the general mindset, as drawn from interviews with officers and civilian decisionmakers, showed a very cautious perspective. After all, there was no reason to predict the fall of Assad as the Israel-Syria border had been quiet since the 1973 war. In other words, it was better to cope with a "devil that you know than with one you don't."[83] But the realization that the Syria problem was not a purely internal crisis that could be contained and disconnected from regional dynamics led Israelis to reevaluate the risks of escalation, in particular as the involvement of Iran and Hezbollah on the Syrian battlefield increased.

Starting in the fall of 2012, Israeli officials emphasized the fact that they considered any transfer of Syrian advanced weaponry to a third party to be a game changer in the Syrian crisis. A Hezbollah armed with Syrian chemical weapons or mid-range ballistic missiles raises the level of vulnerability of Israel's territory and eventually defies the status quo. This rationale has been put to the test more and more, and has led to concrete military action at least twice. While the Golan Heights have been the theater of several skirmishes over several months, it is the January 30 Israeli airstrike in Jamraya, deep inside Syrian territory, that refreshed the prospects of a regionalization of the Syrian battlefield and the reopening of the Lebanese front. The Israeli strike allegedly targeted a convoy of weapons being transferred to Hezbollah. According to several Western media, the weapons included the

Buk-M2 (SA-17 Grizzly) mobile medium-range anti-aircraft system.[84] For other media like the Saudi newspaper, *Al Watan*, the convoy may even have contained chemical weapons.[85]

Following this operation, all parties showed restraint, but it remains to be seen for how long this shaky balance can prevail. In fact, as counterintuitive it may seem, the Israeli strike attempted to contain the crisis to the Syrian territory rather than to regionalize it. In other words, it can be read as a means to disconnect the Syrian front from the Lebanese one. It aimed at maintaining the deterrence system between Israeli forces and Hezbollah that is effective as long as it remains isolated from other theaters in the Middle East.

However, the more Hezbollah gets bogged down in Syria, the more the disconnection between the two fronts is difficult to sustain. This was evidenced a second time in the night between Saturday, May 4, and Sunday, May 5, 2013, when Israeli jets conducted a new raid over the Damascus suburbs in order to destroy arms supplies. This time, according to Western intelligence sources, "What was attacked were stores of Fateh-110 missiles that were in transit from Iran to Hezbollah."[86] The scope of this second air operation was wider, targets including at least three sites, among them the exact same compound in Jamraya as on January 30. Although Hezbollah, as well as Syrian and Iranian regimes, were more vocal in their condemnation of this second raid, it did not trigger a new escalation step.

To be sure, if Hezbollah was to acquire chemical weapons or improved air defense means, the deterrence equilibrium with Israel might be altered. However, the idea of Syria transferring such systems in the middle of its civil war is questionable. The rationale for Assad to give Hezbollah an arsenal that he needs to express his own resolve to deter foreign intervention is shallow. Even regarding the Party of God itself, it postulates that the organization would be ready to gamble on Israel's restraint in front of such transfer. If necessary, the two air strikes conveyed the message that the Israelis would not accept a change in the military equation on their northern front. Additionally, some observers argue that Hezbollah has been fabricating its own rocket arsenal "for at least 4-5 years" in order to decrease its reliance on Syrian supply lines.[87]

But the rationality of each actor cannot predict solely the regional dynamics of the Syrian conflict. The more the crisis extends to the Middle East, the more the strategic balance becomes precarious and the greater the likelihood of misperceptions leading to ill-advised, potentially disastrous decisions. Moreover, with Assad's fight for survival, Hezbollah, just like Iran, is facing what Glenn Snyder calls the "security dilemma in alliance politics:" the more an alliance strengthens the ties and solidarity among its members, the more these are vulnerable to reckless decisions from one of them.[88]

However, at the time of writing this research, the grammar of the Israel-Hezbollah deterrence game remained solid despite the Syrian crisis. The real change in the calculus of all sides is the geography of their competition: The risk of escalation is prevented as long as the clashes involving the various actors are situated inside Syria and limited to its territory. This is an important development that can be compared to the way Lebanon became the buffer zone between Israel and Syria and Iran during its civil war. All during the Lebanese civil war, the regional players drew new redlines, using proxies and delimiting certain areas of influences. As the conflict lasts in Syria, we may be witnessing the same evolution.

Deciphering Lebanese Politics.

As discussed in the previous section, the deterrence equation between Israel and Hezbollah also relies on the ability of the latter to maintain the current status quo within Lebanon regarding its military power. In many ways, distinguishing between Hezbollah's Lebanese politics and regional strategies is arbitrary, as Lebanese politics have historically been driven by the competing agendas of its neighbors — Israel and Syria — but also those of regional players — Iran, Saudi Arabia, Qatar, and Western powers of the United States and France. As a Beirut-insider joked, "the essence of being a Lebanese politician is to be someone else's proxy."[89]

The current tensions in Lebanon over Hezbollah's military support to the Syrian regime of Bashar al-Assad did not suddenly come to light with the Syrian crisis, they had been looming for several years. In fact, one could say that the sectarian character of on-going disputes and fights in Lebanon is reminiscent of the civil war and the loosely stable political system that emerged from these years, with the Taef agreements signed in 1989. The question of Hezbollah's arms might have been dormant during the Israeli occupation, but in the years that followed, the Party went under growing pressure from its multiple Sunni and Christian opponents in Beirut that considered its arsenal to undermine the building of a genuine Lebanese military.

In 2005, the Syrian withdrawal from Lebanon was believed to be a tipping point that would lead to the disarming of the Party. However the war of 2006 only adjourned the major internal crisis which eventually ensued in 2008 with the Sunni-Shia clashes in Beirut.

Like all post-civil war settlements in Lebanon, the Doha agreement signed that same year was more or a less a way to perpetuate the bargain between all the political forces.

In that perspective, the uprisings in Syria did not alter Lebanese politics, they reminded and reinforced the fundamental fault lines of the political game in Beirut. Because of the Syrian military presence in Lebanon for 3 decades, political identities in the country were driven by loyalty or opposition to Damascus. Therefore, it was natural that the Syrian civil war would itself reemphasize these latent divides inside Lebanon. At first, Prime Minister Najib Mikati tried to "dissociate" the country from the Syrian predicament, which meant no foreign policy position taken on the issue. More or less, this dissociation policy was a deliberate attempt to prolong Lebanon's state of denial. For several months, Mikati may have hoped that it would help him balance between Hezbollah and the movement of Saad Hariri.

But in spite of the government's attempt, the country was not immune to the battle between pro-Syria and anti-Syria camps. Starting in the spring of 2012, the city of Tripoli in North Lebanon, the eastern region of the Bekaa, and South-Lebanon became the theaters of repeated clashes between the two camps with the Lebanese Army proving unable to restore order. In July 2012, Sheikh Assir, Salafist leader and imam of the Bilal Bin Rabah Mosque in Sidon, decided to launch a blockade of the city, the capital of the South governorate of Lebanon, to demand the disarmament of Hezbollah.

Then, in mid-August 2012, the arrest of former minister of Information Michel Samaha, accused of plotting a terrorist attack in Northern Lebanon and allegedly taking direct orders from Damascus, reminded the Lebanese of the long Syrian interference in their internal affairs. It was followed in October by a spectacular terrorist attack in the middle of Beirut that targeted Wissam Al Hassan, head of police information, and closely involved in the prosecution of Samaha. In the following months, there were numerous cases of intra-sect confrontations, which only grew as Hezbollah's support to Assad became obvious.

In the context of Lebanese politics, whether or not Assad remains in power is no longer the central question. In any case, Hezbollah will have to make do with a decreasingly reliable regional ally. A major issue for the movement is to preserve what is left of Hezbollah's long process of Lebanonization under Nasrallah's leadership in the 1990s, a process which has been weakened by the political crises of 2005, 2008, and those occurring today. Thus, in other words, Hezbollah's endurance after a collapse of the Assad regime does not depend exclusively on its arsenal but on the reactions of its constituency and the evolving balance with its rivals in Beirut.

The anti-Syria camp of Saad Hariri has publicly embraced the cause of Syrian rebels and aims at capitalizing on the crisis as a game changer vis-à-vis Hezbollah. Christian and Druze leaders have been in a much more ambiguous situation. The Christian allies of Hezbollah, the followers of General Michel Aoun, are not at ease with Hezbollah's full support of Assad. But on the other side, the Christians associated with Hariri eye with concern the steady rise of Sunni fundamentalism and jihadism with the fighters crossing the border to Syria from the Tripoli area.

As proven by the history of Lebanon's politics, each of the political players is likely to change its calculus rapidly and rebalance the distribution of power among the competing blocs, depending on the perceived outcome of the Syrian war. But eventually this does not challenge Hezbollah's power militarily. The Salafis led by Sheikh Assir may be a nuisance in the South, but they do not compete militarily with Hezbollah. Even the Lebanese Army does not constitute a serious competitor to the military power of the Party. It does not possess a comparable arsenal, but it is itself a divided institution that reflects the sectarian rivalries in the country. In other words, if Hezbollah's efforts were to result in loss, it would be due less to its military strength capabilities — again sufficient enough to maintain the movement, even in the face of Israel or any Lebanese rival — but on its political support, and more particularly on its future ability to defuse the impact of the Syrian crisis in the on-going Lebanese Sunni-Shia rivalries to avoid the organization's complete alienation from Beirut's political scene.

For Israel, the paradox is that, although in the long term, it would appreciate the fall of Hezbollah, in the short term, it may prefer a strong Hezbollah that maintains its hold on south Lebanon and its control over its arsenal. This is the ultimate dimension of the deterrence system shaped by both actors since 2006: The more they rely on this calculus, the more they depend on the relative strength of the other to preserve this strategic stability.

Another element of the equation that needs to be considered is the uncertain future of the UNIFIL. Since 2006, the expanded UNIFIL has been seen as successfully preserving the peace in South Lebanon. Compared to average peacekeeping operations, the number of contributing nations (38), as well as the overall number of troops (11,000), reflects the commitment of the international community. But today, the elements that helped UNIFIL perform its mission are turning against them. The first issue putting the future of UNIFIL at risk is the more visible assertiveness of Hezbollah vis-à-vis the peacekeepers in the South. Pragmatism prevailed, and there was an implicit division of labor, according to which UNIFIL forces were able to monitor certain areas, while letting Hezbollah maintain its hold in others.

This compromise worked until late-2011, but since then, there have been numerous cases of interference between the UN forces and the Party of God. For instance, officers referred to blocked patrols in areas where they previously experienced no issue.[90] The assertiveness of Hezbollah in the South is not new by itself, but its scale is. This deterioration in the UNIFIL-Hezbollah bargain may be Hezbollah's way to remind both UNIFIL and Israel that despite its engagement in Syria, its forces remain focused on South Lebanon as their key battleground.

In July 2013, the European Union (EU) officially put the military wing of Hezbollah on its list of terrorist organizations. Some officials in France and Italy feared that this recent European move to antagonize Hezbollah's role along the forces of Bashar al-Assad against the rebels could exacerbate the difficulties of UNIFIL. It started on Tuesday, May 21, when the United Kingdom (UK) formally requested that the EU add the military wing of Hezbollah to its list of terrorist organizations. London had been pushing for this change in the EU policy for several months, as details of Hezbollah's criminal activities surfaced in Europe earlier this year.[91] The major difference from previous British attempts is that France and Germany, two countries long considered to accommodate with Hezbollah, support the initiative.

One country expressed caution but in vain: Italy, which is commanding UNIFIL. Rome was irritated by the absence of any prior European coordination and assessment concerning the potential repercussions of the British initiative on European forces in Lebanon, which represent nine of the contributing nations. Consequently, Hezbollah's assertiveness in the South may be an indirect way to deter the Europeans from targeting its involvement in Syria.

The second issue affecting the future of UNIFIL is the level of cooperation with the Lebanese armed forces. A key objective in 2006 was to "accompany and support the Lebanese armed forces as they deploy throughout the South."[92] But today it is estimated that only 10 percent of UNIFIL patrols are conducted jointly with Lebanese troops.[93] In fact, the clashes in the northern part of the country, particularly in Tripoli, between pro-Assad and anti-Assad forces have led to a redeployment of the Lebanese soldiers from south to north. The consequence for UNIFIL is that its mission is less about supporting the Lebanese State than merely playing its role.

One could argue that the purpose of UNIFIL is still relevant and that no regional player has any interest in seeing them leave. Both Israel and Hezbollah want to avoid a flare-up in the Lebanese theater. But one other big issue that is less understood is the slow but steady decline in UNIFIL size on the ground as a result of its safety and its financial burden. Whereas UNIFIL was supposed to comprise 15,000 men in 2006, it never went above 13,500 and now numbers 11,000.

For the Europeans, the drawdown has already started: European countries represented more than 60 percent of UNIFIL contingents in 2006, they now constitute only 30 percent of the peacekeepers. These cuts in manpower result mainly from the European financial crisis, but the rising problems of safety for the peacekeepers also play a role. This was evidenced by Spain, a long-time key contributor that substantially lowered its participation. France and Italy also decreased their share of the burden and, according to insiders in Rome and Paris, it could go down even more. The result is that the more the Europeans leave the leadership of UNIFIL, the more the high number of contributing nations becomes an unmanageable liability.

For all these reasons, in the coming months, UNIFIL could reach a threshold below which its strategic credibility would be compromised. Particularly, the political clout of UNIFIL without the Europeans would diminish. Since 2006, UNIFIL command has only been assigned to France, Spain, and Italy. Indonesia, now the biggest contributor to UNIFIL, already made the claim to command the forces but in vain, because there is a common understanding among the UN Secretariat, Israel, and Lebanon that the credibility of UNIFIL relies primarily on European political and military commitment. The fact that Indonesia has no diplomatic relations with Israel also means that an Indonesian commander would merely have no influence.

The scholar might be tempted to argue that the withdrawal of UNIFIL forces or their near-complete irrelevance in the Israel-Hezbollah game would be the ultimate way to measure the deterrence factor as the prevailing one in the stability of the area. However, the very risks of a new conflict may not be worth exploring such scenario in practice.

Coping with Iranian Nuclear Opacity.

The third trigger for a shift in the Israel-Hezbollah deterrence equation is the acquisition by the Iranian regime of nuclear weapons. Indeed, as the several rounds of talks between Western powers and Tehran failed to reach a diplomatic breakthrough, the likelihood of a nuclear-armed Iran is still significant. As of today, there is no undeniable evidence that Iran is seeking nuclear weapons, but there are many plausible signs that its program is not serving solely civilian purposes.

Because a nuclear-armed Iran would challenge the military escalation in the Middle East, it is worth exploring the ramifications of such scenario, in particular with regards to the Israel-Hezbollah competition. The characteristics of an Iranian nuclear deterrent will depend, first, on the advent of its nuclear program in the military domain, whether Iran manufactures deliverable or only unassembled nuclear weapons; second, on the quantity and quality of its delivery systems; and third, on the inclusion of nuclear weapons in Iran's strategic culture. Several scholars interpret the modern Iranian international posture as the expression of Persian history and identity that combines a sense of superiority over its neighbors with a deep sense of insecurity.[94] As a result, academic studies have usually evoked Iranian strategic culture to argue that Iran is a rational actor rather than an irrational and unpredictable religiously fanatic state.[95]

One critical unknown in such scenario is the role that Iran would confer to nuclear weapons in both its competition with Israel and its patronage of Hezbollah. The Iranian decision may test the status quo between the IDF and Hezbollah, providing the latter with a new precious psychological advantage.

Still, the question of Iran's security guarantees to its allies or proxies is not obvious and cannot be answered only by discussing the relevance of formal guarantees. A fair share of experts on the topic asserts that a nuclear-armed Iran would not change the Israel-Hezbollah equation because the Iranian leadership would by no means risk their country to support the Lebanese movement. Shashank Joshi from the Royal United Service Institute (RUSI) writes that:

> [This scenario] would be as if Slobodan Milosevic had threatened NATO [The North Atlantic Treaty Organization] with Russian nuclear attack during the Kosovo War of 1999. Only if Iran made a concerted effort to extend deterrence over Hezbollah would such a declaration carry weight, but this means returning to the question of why Iran would take risks so disproportionate to its interests.[96]

But the relation between Iran and Hezbollah cannot strictly be analyzed through analogies taken from alliances between states. First, at the military level, many Israeli scholars and military planners tend to see Hezbollah as closely linked to the Iranian Revolutionary Guards in a way that transcends a mere proxy-patron relation. Accordingly, the Iranian Revolutionary Guards would be involved at all levels of Hezbollah's military structure. This obviously questions the level of autonomy of the Lebanese organization vis-à-vis the Iranian regime in terms of decision-making. For instance, in January 2005, Major General Jafari ambiguously claimed that "in addition to its own capabilities, Iran has also excellent deterrence capabilities outside its [own borders] and if necessary it will utilize them."[97] Although it has been argued that Hezbollah was primarily a Lebanese organization, the fact that the first vision prevails in the Israeli defense community has implications on the way the escalation process would be understood by the IDF.[98]

Second, at the political level, it is often forgotten that Iran's and Hezbollah's leaders share a feeling of common destiny that goes beyond state-to-nonstate interactions. Ties between Hassan Nasrallah or the late Mohammad Hussein Fadlallah (the spiritual guide of Hezbollah) and the religious and political leaders in Tehran date back to the 1960s and 1970s when they were all students at the Shia School of Najaf in Iraq.[99] These ties are not only spiritual, they are political but yet refer to a kinship that is not state-centered. They refer to the old concept of Ibn Khaldoun of *'asabiyya* that designates solidarity in a social group based on the sense of shared purpose and *esprit de corps*.[100]

These elements mean that Hezbollah would benefit, at least symbolically, from the uncertainty associated to Iran's involvement in the crisis. It could exploit this opacity in various ways. As a nonstate actor, it could play the game of calculated irrationality. In his seminal book, *On Escalation*, Herman Kahn detailed the logic of such behavior:

> In most deterrent situations, once deterrence has failed it is irrational to carry out the previously made warnings or threats of retaliation since that action will produce an absolute or net loss to the retaliator. Thus the threat of retaliation, in order to be believable, must depend upon the potential irrationality of the retaliator.[101]

As a result, in the midst of a conflict, an emotional, out-of-control threat of an overwhelming but unspecified retaliation issued by Hassan Nasrallah could convey the intended impression of irrationality that would deter the IDF.[102] Hezbollah could also show great confidence during the confrontation if it assumed (rightly or wrongly) that Iran would undoubtedly back it up in the event of escalation. However, even if the IDF had evidence that Iran was supporting Hezbollah's adventurism, they would have to maintain a disconnection between the two fronts. To that aim, they might have to refrain from directly attacking Iranian targets and limit the scope of their retaliation to Hezbollah targets in order to avoid uncontrolled escalation. Unless Tehran offered a formal pledge regarding nuclear protection of its proxies (which is unlikely), Israel would have to operate in an uncertain environment where the fault lines for escalation would be unknown and, as a result, extremely difficult to control. In a nutshell, nuclear opacity works here as a miscalculation multiplier. Israel may attempt to disconnect the Hezbollah challenge from the Iranian front the same way it is doing with the Syrian front. However, the major difference is that whereas Hezbollah has an objective interest in disconnecting the Lebanese and Syrian fronts, it also benefits from assimilating its fight with Israel to the Iranian nuclear ambitions. It raises the costs, either military or at least psychological, of an IDF intervention against the Party of God.

All in all, the deterrence game that prevailed until recently between Israel and Hezbollah is likely to be put under serious tests in the coming years. The volatility of the regional environment is reflected in the developments in Lebanon, Iran, and Syria. But when push comes to shove, the question remains the same: In the name of which logic could Hezbollah or Israel decide to end the cold peace that lasted since 2006? This relates to a deeper unknown: How long can the rationalities of both Israel and Hezbollah match each other in order to prevent a new conflict? As we have seen in this monograph, both have different approaches to deterrence, making the relative stability of the region for the last 8 years even more bewildering.

CONCLUSION

The findings of this monograph have implications for both scholars and practitioners. First, the history of Israel-Hezbollah competition since the 2006 war is a revealing case on the making of a deterrence system between two adversaries. It highlights the role of arms race—both offensive and defensive means—to create a kind of "balance of terror," as well as the importance of public messages and declaratory policies—as seen through the Israeli *Dahya* concept or Hezbollah's propaganda.

In the meantime, this case also stresses the precariousness of any deterrence system. The stand-off between Israel and Hezbollah reached this level only through specific measures and conditions that can be reversed in the future. In particular, exogenous factors such as the unraveling of the Syrian civil war or the developments of the Iranian nuclear issue can jeopardize the equilibrium. Moreover, the study of Lebanese politics emphasizes the uncertainties related to the logic of deterrence with a non-state actor like Hezbollah. This is why this analysis aimed at offering a cautious look at deterrence theories in the Middle East by reminding that such situations are neither naturally engendered nor eternally established.

This also matters for the practitioners in the U.S. national security community. This monograph ventured in particular to explain the potential ramifications of the crisis in Syria and the Iranian conundrum over the Israel-Hezbollah struggle. We have seen, for instance, that Israeli air strikes in Syria in the spring of 2013 did not intend to escalate the conflict, but rather to disconnect it from the Lebanese theater. Likewise, the current and future role of missiles and rockets in Hezbollah's strategic culture gives an important meaning to American-Israeli cooperation in the field of missile defense system.

The understanding of all the implicit rules of the game in this deterrence system may prove crucial for U.S. decisionmakers when addressing the on-going events. If a conflict was to occur again in the Levant, and given the readiness of both parties, it is likely to be wider in its scale than the 2006 war. This is the very reason why the U.S. Government needs to be fully aware of the inner logic of this conflict, in order if necessary to rapidly identify the ways to deescalate the latter.

ENDNOTES

1. Daniel Byman, "Israel's Pessimistic View of the Arab Spring," *The Washington Quarterly*, Vol. 34, No. 3, Summer 2011, pp. 123-136.

2. Paul Nitze, "Assuring strategic stability in an era of dé-tente," *Foreign Affairs*, Vol. 54, No. 2, January 1976, p. 207.

3. For a recent assessment of deterrence in the Israeli context, see Thomas Rid, "Deterrence beyond the State: The Israeli Experience," *Contemporary Security Policy*, Vol. 33, No. 1, April 2012, pp. 124-147.

4. Ben Gurion is said to have made the statement as advice given to Ariel Sharon, then Special Forces commander in the Israeli Army. Quote from Daniel Byman, *A High Price: The Triumphs and Failures of Israeli Counterterrorism*, Oxford, UK: Oxford University Press, 2011, p. 1.

5. Moshe Dayan, "Why Israel Strikes Back," Donald Robinson, *Under Fire: Israel's Twenty Years Struggle for Survival*, New York: Norton, 1968, p. 122.

6. Interviews conducted by the author with Israeli officers in Tel Aviv, Israel, February 2013.

7. Doron Almog, "Cumulative Deterrence and the War on Terrorism," *Parameters*, Vol. 34, No. 1, Winter 2004-05, pp. 4-19, especially p. 8.

8. *Ibid.*, p. 9.

9. Interview conducted by the author, Tel Aviv.

10. Interview conducted by the author with Uri Bar-Joseph in Tel Aviv, February 2013.

11. Yoav Ben-Horin and Barry Posen, *Israel's Strategic Doctrine*, Santa Monica, CA: RAND Corporation, 1981, p. 12.

12. Uri Bar-Joseph, "Variations on a Theme: The Conceptualization of Deterrence in Israeli Strategic Thinking," *Security Studies*, Vol. 7, No. 3, Spring 1998, pp. 145-181, especially p.147.

13. A. Nizar Hamzeh, "Lebanon's Hezbollah: from Islamic revolution to parliamentary accommodation," *Third World Quarterly*, Vol. 14, No. 2, Spring 1993, pp. 321-337; Augustus Richard Norton, "Hizballah: from radicalism to pragmatism?" *Middle East Policy*, Vol. 5, No. 4, January 1998, pp. 147-158.

14. Interview with Hassan Nasrallah in Nicholas Noe, ed., *Voice of Hezbollah: The Statements of Sayyed Hassan Nasrallah*, London, UK: Verso, 2007, p. 63.

15. Quoted in Noe, p. 62.

16. Daniel Sobelman, *New Rules of the Game: Israel and Hizbollah after the Withdrawal from Lebanon*, Tel Aviv, Israel: Jaffee Center for Strategic Studies, January 2004, p. 80.

17. Among others, see the illustrative book by Youssef Nas-rallah, *Psychological warfare: Essays on the strategy of Hezbolla* (Al Harb An Nasfyah: Kara'at fi Istrategyat Hezbollah), Beirut, Leba-non: Dar Alfarabi, 2012; Hassan Mahmoud Qabissi, *The Fall and the Defeat* (Al Inhidar wa al Indihar), Beirut, Lebanon: Mou'assat al 'Aroua al Wathaqa, 2010.

18. Hassan Nasrallah, Speech at the Festival of Victory in Bint Jbeil City, May 26, 2000, available from *english.alahednews.com.lb/ essaydetails.php?eid=14178&cid=446#.UbCiTcqEkik.*

19. One could argue that, during the Suez crisis of 1956, the Israeli Air Force (IAF) did achieve decisive military results but failed at the political level, following the international condemna-tion of the operation.

20. Yoaz Hendel, "Failed Tactical Intelligence in the Lebanon War," *Strategic Assessment*, Vol. 9, No. 3, November 2006, avail-able from *d26e8pvoto2x3r.cloudfront.net/uploadImages/systemFiles/ AdkanEng9_3_Hendel.pdf.*

21. Raphael Cohen-Almagor and Sharon Haleva-Amir, "The Israel-Hezbollah War And The Winograd Committee," *Journal of Parliamentary and Political Law*, Vol. 2, No. 1, December 2008, pp. 27-44, especially p. 32.

22. Harel, p. 45.

23. On this narrative, see Or Honig, "The End of Israeli Mili-tary Restraint: Out with the New, in with the Old," *Middle East Quarterly*, Vol. 14, No. 1, Winter 2007, pp. 63-74.

24. International Institute for Strategic Studies, *The Military Balance 2008*, London, UK: Routledge, p. 230.

25. Yotam Feldman, "Dr. Naveh, or, how I learned to stop worrying and walk through walls," *Haaretz*, October 25, 2007.

26. Interview conducted by the author with Israeli officers, in Tel Aviv, Israel, February 2013.

27. Avi Kober, "The Israel defense forces in the Second Lebanon War: Why the poor performance?" *Journal of Strategic Studies*, Vol. 31, No. 1, February 2008, pp. 3-40, especially p.32.

28. Amir Rapaport, "The IDF and the Lessons of the Second Lebanon War," Mideast Security and Policy Studies, No. 85, Ramat Gan, Israel: Begin-Sadat Center for Strategic Studies, December 2010, p. 4.

29. Ron Tira, "Breaking the Amoeba's Bones," *Strategic Assessment*, Vol. 9, No. 3, November 2006.

30. Amos Harel and Avi Issacharoff, *34 Days: Israel, Hezbollah, and the War in Lebanon*, New York: Palgrave, 2009, p. 103.

31. Interview conducted by the author with an Israeli officer, Tel Aviv.

32. Kober, "The Israel defense forces in the Second Lebanon War," p. 22.

33. "Israel warns Hezbollah war would invite destruction," *Yedioth Ahronoth*, October 3, 2008, available from *www.ynetnews.com/articles/0,7340,L-3604893,00.html*.

34. For a detailed analysis of the urban growth of Hezbollah's neighborhoods, see Mona Harb, *Le Hezbollah à Beyrouth (1985-2005): De la banlieue à la ville*, Paris, France: Karthala, 2010.

35. Interview conducted by the author with an Israeli defense journalist in Tel Aviv, Israel, February 2012.

36. Gabi Siboni, "Disproportionate Force: Israel's Concept of Response in Light of the Second Lebanon War," *INSS Insight*, No. 74, October 2, 2008, available from *www.inss.org.il/index.aspx?id=4538&articleid=1964*.

37. Giora Eiland, "The Third Lebanon War: Target Lebanon," *Strategic Assessment*, Vol. 11, No. 2, November 2008, pp. 9-17, especially p.16.

38. United Nations Human Rights Council, *Report of the United Nations Fact Finding Mission on the Gaza Conflict*, New York, No. 15, September 2009, p. 331.

39. Interviews conducted by the author with Israeli officers, Tel Aviv.

40. Phone Interview conducted by the author with Gabi Siboni, March 29, 2012.

41. The most illustrative case of this commonsensical view is Scott C. Farquhar, ed., *Back to Basics: A Study of the Second Lebanon War and Operation CAST LEAD*, Ft. Leavenworth, KS: Combat Studies Institute Press, U.S. Army Combined Arms Center, 2009. For a critical assessment of this narrative, see Lazar Berman, "Beyond the Basics: Looking Beyond the Conventional Wisdom Surrounding the IDF Campaigns against Hizbullah and Hamas," *Small Wars Journal*, April 28, 2011.

42. Gadi Eisenkot, "A Changed Threat? The Response on the Northern Arena," *Military and Strategic Affairs*, Vol. 2, No. 1, June 2010, pp. 29-40, especially p. 29.

43. Eisenkot, "Israel's Security in the 21st Century," p. 10.

44. Giora Eiland, "The Third Lebanon War," *Strategic Assessment*, Vol. 11, No. 2, November 2008, pp. 9-17, especially p. 12.

45. Gabriel Siboni, "From the Second Intifada through the Second Lebanon War to Operation Cast Lead: Puzzle Pieces of a Single Campaign," *Military and Strategic Affairs*, Vol. 1, No. 1, April 2009, pp. 25-33, especially p. 26.

46. "Eizenkot: Rocket defenses designed for IDF, not citizens," *Jerusalem Post*, December 12, 2010.

47. During the November 2012 campaign in the Gaza Strip, Iron Dome achieved a success rate of 85 percent. For decision-makers, numbers matter and, in this case, they lent full support to the case for missile defense: Of the 1,506 rockets fired at Israel, only 58 fell in urban areas.

48. Yaakov Katz, "Signs of the Times," *Jerusalem Post*, February 3, 2012.

49. On the political consequences of the war, see Paul Salem, "The after effects of the 2006 Israel–Hezbollah war," *Contemporary Arab Affairs*, Vol. 1, No. 1, 2008, pp. 15-24.

50. There is no official number of casualties for Hezbollah fighters during the 2006 war. Although the leadership of the Party declared that 250 men died fighting, Israeli authorities claim that the real number is closer to 600.

51. Stephen D. Biddle and Jeffrey A. Friedman, *The 2006 Lebanon Campaign and the Future of Warfare: Implications for Army and Defense Policy*, Carlisle, PA: Strategic Studies Institute, U.S. Army War College, 2008, p. xv.

52. "Hezbollah chief Nasrallah refuses to disarm," Associated Press, September 22, 2006.

53. See Youssef Nasrallah, 2012; Hassan Mahmoud Qabissi, 2010.

54. Houda Kassatly, "Des interventions surnaturelles à la victoire divine, le merveilleux dans les récits de la guerre de 33 jours" ("From extraordinary interventions to divine victory, the supernatural in the narratives of the 33 day war"), Sabrina Mervin, ed., *Le Hezbollah état des lieux*, Paris, France: Actes Sud, 2008.

55. Blanford, p. 435.

56. Ari Rabinovitch, "Israel's Barak Warns of Growing Hezbollah Arsenal," *Reuters*, September 10, 2008; Avi Issacharaoff, "Peres: Israel Knows Hezbollah Has 80,000 Rockets," *Haaretz*, August 24, 2009.

57. Interviews conducted by the author with Israeli officers, Tel Aviv.

58. Charles Levinson and Jay Solomon, "Syria Gave Scuds to Hezbollah, U.S. Says," *The Wall Street Journal*, April 14, 2010.

59. Blanford, p. 433.

60. "The Final Hours of Imad Mughniyeh," *Al Akhbar*, February 19, 2013.

61. Hassan Nasrallah, Speech on the 6th Anniversary of the "Divine Victory," available from *english.alahednews.com.lb/essaydetails.php?eid=20566&cid=361&st=Divine Victory*.

62. Casey Addis and Christopher Blanchard, "Hezbollah: Background and Issues for Congress," Washington, DC: Congressional Research Service, 2011, pp. 16-17.

63. Mark Landler, "U.S. Speaks to Syrian Envoy of Arms Worries," *New York Times*, April 19, 2010.

64. Jeffrey White, *If War Comes: Israel vs. Hizballah and Its Allies*, Washington, DC: Washington Institute for Near East Policy, September 2010, p. 20.

65. Blanford and Saab, p. 9.

66. Addis and Blanchard, p. 10.

67. Amnon Meranda, "Military Intelligence: Hezbollah Scuds tip of iceberg," *Ynetnews.com*, May 4, 2010.

68. Interview conducted by the author with a policy advisor to the French Minister of Defense, in Paris, France, May 2013.

69. Resolution 1701 adopted by the United Nations Security Council, August 11, 2006, p. 2.

70. Available from *www.washingtonpost.com/wp-srv/special/world/Israeli-military-information-on-Hezbollah.html*.

71. Hassan Nasrallah, *Khitaab al radaa'*, DVD Video, Dar Al Manar, Beirut, Lebanon, 2010.

72. Daniel Meier, "Mleeta : le Hezbollah en musée" ("Mleeta: Hezbollah's Museum"), *Les Carnets de l'Ifpo. La recherche en train de se faire à l'Institut français du Proche-Orient, Hypotheses.org*, May 3, 2012, available from *ifpo.hypotheses.org/3385*.

73. Blanford and Saab, p. 10.

74. Mariam Karouny, "Nasrallah Threatens Ships Going to Israel in Future War," *Reuters*, May 25, 2010.

75. On the issue of chain of command and deterrence, see (among others) Peter Feaver, "Command and Control in Emerging Nuclear Nations," *International Security*, Vol. 17, No. 3, Winter 1992-93, pp. 160-187.

76. Amal Saad-Ghorayeb, *In Their Own Words: Hizbollah's Strategy in the Current Confrontation*, Beirut, Lebanon: Carnegie Endowment for International Peace, 2007, p. 12.

77. "Beirut to axe Hezbollah telecoms," *BBC*, May 6, 2008.

78. International Crisis Group, "Lebanon: Hizbollah's Weapons Turn Inward," *Middle East Briefing*, No. 23, May 15, 2008, p. 2.

79. Richard Ned Lebow and Janice Gross Stein, *When Does Deterrence Succeed and How Do We Know It?* Ontario, Canada: Canadian Institute for International Peace and Security, 1990.

80. "Nasrallah you'azi al qada al shuhada fi Suria wa rifaqi assilah" ("Nasrallah mourns the leaders martyrs in Syria and brothers in arms"), *Anaharnet*, August 20, 2012.

81. Farnaz Fassihi, "Iran Said to Send Troops to Bolster Syria," *Wall Street Journal*, August 27, 2012; Marcus George, "Iran's Revolutionary Guards commander says its troops in Syria," *Reuters*, September 16, 2012.

82. "Nasrallah you`akidou istikmal al maarakat haithou yajib an nakounou fi Souria" ("Nasrallah stresses the importance of the battle where we need to be in Syria"), *Anaharnet,* June 14, 2013.

83. Interviews conducted by the author with representatives of Israeli Ministry of Defense and Ministry of Foreign Affairs, Tel Aviv and Jerusalem, Israel, January 2012.

84. Nicholas Blanford, "Enemy at the gates," *Jane's Intelligence Review*, April 2013, p. 8.

85. Khalid Al Owigan, "Al Watan Taktashifou Naql Al Assad Assliha Kimawouya li Hezbollah" ("Al Watan Discovers Al Assad's Transfer of Chemical Weapons to Hezbollah"), *Al Watan*, January 30, 2013.

86. Dominic Evans and Oliver Holmes, "Israel strikes Syria, says targeting Hezbollah arms," *Reuters*, May 5, 2013.

87. Nicholas Noe, "Hizbullah's expanding military involvement in Syria and the reduction of the supply line threat," *The Mideastwire Blog*, February 18, 2013.

88. Glenn Snyder, *Alliance Politics*, Ithaca, NY: Cornell University Press, 1997, pp. 182-183.

89. Interview conducted by the author with a Lebanese politician, in Beirut, Lebanon, July 2012.

90. Nicholas Blanford, "UNIFIL increasingly frustrated with Hezbollah," *The Daily Star*, May 1, 2013.

91. In February 2013, the Bulgarian government announced that two of the individuals responsible for the July 2012 bombing at the Burgas Airport that killed five Israeli tourists and a Bulgarian bus driver "belonged to the military formation of Hezbollah." This came around the same time that Cyprus prosecuted a Lebanese-Swedish citizen who had confessed to be a Hezbollah operative watching Israeli tourists as potential targets.

92. Resolution 1701 adopted by the United Nations Security Council, August 11, 2006, p. 2.

93. Nicholas Blanford, "UNIFIL increasingly frustrated with Hezbollah," *The Daily Star*, May 1, 2013.

94. Gregory F. Giles, "The Crucible of Radical Islam: Iran's Leaders and Strategic Culture," Barry R. Schneider and Jerrold M. Post, eds., *Know Thy Enemy: Profiles of Adversary Leaders and Their Strategic Cultures*, Maxwell Air Force Base, AL: USAF Counterproliferation Center, 2003, pp. 141-162, especially p. 146.

95. Anthony C. Cain, *Iran's Strategic Culture and Weapons of Mass Destruction: Implications of US Policy*, Maxwell Paper No. 26, Montgomery, AL: Air War College, April 2002, p. 16.

96. Shashank Joshi, *The Permanent Crisis: Iran's Nuclear Trajectory*, London, UK: Routledge, 2012, p. 92.

97. Sabahat Khan, *Strategies in Contemporary Maritime Security: Challenges Confronting the Arabian Gulf*, Dubai, United Arab Emirates: Institute for Near East and Gulf Military Analysis, 2009, p. 35.

98. Interviews conducted by the author with Israel officers, Tel Aviv.

99. Sabrina Mervin, "La quête du savoir à Najaf. Les études religieuses chez les chiites imamites de la fin du XIXe siècle à 1960" ("The search for wisdom in Najaf. Religious studies among the Shiite Imams from the end of the XIXth century to 1960"), *Studia Islamica*, Vol. 85, No. 1, 1995, pp. 165-185.

100. Ibn Khaldun, *The Muqaddimah: An Introduction to History*, Princeton, NJ: Princeton University Press, 2004. See a modern use of *'asabiyya* in Michel Seurat, *Syrie: L'Etat de Barbarie* (*Syria: The State of Barbarism*), Paris, France: PUF, 2012.

101. Herman Kahn, *On Escalation*, London, UK: Pall Mall Press, 1965, pp. 57-58.

102. On the issue of calculated irrationality and nuclear deterrence, see Henry Nash, *Nuclear Weapons and International Behavior*, New York: Springer, 1975, p. 79.

www.ingramcontent.com/pod-product-compliance
Lightning Source LLC
Chambersburg PA
CBHW072013290526
45787CB00013B/888